Seasons in the Word
Liturgical Homilies
Year A

Fr. John Sandell

LITURGICAL PRESS
Collegeville, Minnesota

www.litpress.org

Cover design by Greg Becker. Cover photos © The Crosiers.

Year A: ISBN 0-8146-2592-4
Year B: ISBN 0-8146-2586-X
Year C: ISBN 0-8146-2585-1

2	3	4	5	6	7

Library of Congress Cataloging-in-Publication Data

Sandell, John, 1942–
    Seasons in the Word : liturgical homilies / John Sandell.
        p.   cm.
    Contents: — [2] Year B.
    ISBN 0-8146-2586-X (alk. paper : v. 2)
    1. Church year sermons. 2. Catholic Church—Sermons. I. Title.

BX1756.A2S26 2002
252'.6—dc21

                                            2002067642

Contents

Contents

Contents

First Sunday of Advent

I suppose if there is any one insight into the nature of things that is common to everyone it would have to be that the world is imperfect.

Just experience teaches us that one of the first challenges of human living is to develop an attitude that will allow us to make a certain amount of peace with imperfection. And for centuries human beings have sought for that attitude.

Some of those searchers have concluded that imperfection in the world is simply the way it is. Satisfaction depends on training oneself to live in as small a world as possible, training oneself not to know about imperfection and the suffering it causes or, if awareness is unavoidable, then at least not to care.

But for many others that answer doesn't satisfy. They labor under too strong a conviction that the human condition should be better than it is. Traditionally such as these have been history's visionaries, poets, and prophets.

The first reading today is taken from the writings of just one such visionary, the prophet Isaiah. He was writing for an oppressed people, and yet his vision is one of perfect peace, a vision of a world of people who have beaten their swords into plowshares, people who have no use for weapons.

But in Isaiah's vision it is not humanity that will make the world perfect, it is God. And, in that, Isaiah takes his place among a very special band of visionaries. A band with roots in the earliest covenant of the Old Testament that finds its fullest expression in the visions of Paul, John, and Christ himself.

And in their visions we who are Christians find ourselves confronted with the truth that the God who made the world, who redeemed it and claimed it, will one day return to the world to make it fully his own, to make it perfect.

This morning we begin again the season of Advent, a season in which we reflect on the fact that it is a very Christian thing to learn to wait, with patience, with confidence, and with vigilance.

In the second reading St. Paul speaks about the sacred quality of Christian waiting. Our waiting is a sacred thing because this longed-for coming is something that has already begun. God has already been here in his Son, and he is here now in his Spirit. As we wait for his final coming we must do so very much aware of the opportunities his already present Spirit gives us to hasten the day when Isaiah's vision will be a reality. We are, right now, today, very much involved in the coming of the New Kingdom. Paul calls us to do nothing that will dull our longing for the coming of Christ or mask our awareness of the fact that he is on his way, the way which the great Advent prophet, John the Baptist, urges us to make straight.

Second Sunday of Advent

John the Baptist must have been a strange man. Certainly he was a driven man, and when a person is as strongly driven as that all that is important is that somehow the rest of the world comes to see at least something of what he sees. And what John the Baptist saw was the Holiness of God.

All throughout the Old Testament God makes no secret of his power, or his creativity, or his mercy, or his anger . . . but for his own reasons he seems almost to have kept his holiness masked. Only Moses, and then but briefly, is ever pictured as seeing God face to face.

But John signals the coming of a new relationship between God and his people. And because of that, in John's teaching, there begins to be born a new morality, a morality that demands holiness of human beings, not because the law says so, but simply because God himself is holy, and for his creatures, made in his image, to act in any other way was unthinkable. So for John, the evil of sin was not so much that it caused suffering, or that it merited punishment, but rather that sin is so terribly blasphemous. It is an affront, a violation of the holiness of God, and so of human nature itself.

John the Baptist spoke to a people that had grown very comfortable, very lazy in their spiritual lives, very sure of themselves and the righteousness of their designs. A people that had grown comfortable with sin.

And in that John the Baptist spoke to an age much like our own. We don't like to hear people talk to us about sin. We would much rather try to explain all human suffering, failing, and evil in terms of psychological disorders, social change, pressure, tension, anxiety, and so on.

But to say even all of that is really not to say much. After all, ages, cultures, and societies don't exist. Only people do.

Sin is a very personal and concrete thing. If there is sin in the world it is so not because society fails, or some system somewhere, but rather because you and I, and many others no different from you and I, have allowed ourselves to become foolish, and dull, and selfish. We even like ourselves that way.

We must hear in Advent, then, John's call to purify our lives, a call to regain a sense of the holiness of God, and of the holiness created in us by God. We must bring ourselves to the point where we, like John, are shocked by sin, outraged by it. We must never fall into the trap of letting how comfortable we are with ourselves be the only standard we follow in criticizing our personal morality. In the Gospel those who came to John the Baptist felt very good about themselves, and he called them a brood of vipers whose destruction had already begun.

Third Sunday of Advent

We Christians truly are an Advent people, not only at this time of the year but always. Long after Christmas we will still be an Advent people; we will still be waiting for the return of Christ, the time of which Isaiah writes so joyfully in this first reading today.

It must be a strong element of our faith to constantly be looking forward in hopeful expectation to a new Kingdom in which people will relate to God, to one another, and to all of creation on a new basis.

Because, the truth of the matter is, we are not home yet. Our home is not finished. This world, this society, this Church is still being built.

And that really is something like what it means to say that we are an Advent people. Our world, right now, is temporary. It works pretty well but not nearly as well as it will. Most of the time the situations in which we live provide us with most of what we need to make life possible and pleasant . . . most of the time.

But when it doesn't, when we find ourselves feeling empty and disappointed, perhaps even a little bit betrayed by life, then is the time to remember that it is foolish to expect the world as it now is, people as they now are, to be completely satisfying, completely fulfilling. The kind of world, the kind of society, be it the family, the town, the nation, the Church, that can fully satisfy a creature made in the image of God simply has not yet been created. But it will be. And in the strength of that "will be" the inconvenience of an unfinished world can be so much more easily borne.

So there will be, for now, this kind of tension built in to the experience of being human. A tension between the "already" and the "not yet."

But there is really no great secret to living successfully, even joyfully, with this tension. It is confident patience, nothing more complicated than that. That is what hope is, really, confident patience, and in so many ways it is at the heart of Christian virtue. The patience of Mary. The patience of a person who knows that she has done and is doing all she can to prepare for the end result of a process which she doesn't really understand but which she knows is going well.

The Gospel reading today speaks of John the Baptist in prison, sending his disciples out to ask Christ for reassurance, to ask him, "Really, IS something happening? Is the New Kingdom here?"

And Christ answers, with the imagery of Isaiah to reassure John, to tell him, "Yes, it has begun. Be patient. Happy are those who do not lose faith in me."

Fourth Sunday of Advent

In the gospel, the figure of Joseph offers us a powerful Advent prophecy this weekend.

Joseph's wait was different from that of the others. For him, the reality of God moving in his life was a challenge to his faith, to his patience, to his honor. The movement of God in his life demanded of Joseph radical changes in his attitude toward himself, toward his future, toward the family he hoped to have, even toward the woman he loved and wanted to marry.

She was going to have a baby. And it wasn't his. Marriage now was out of the question. He could denounce her publicly. If he did that he would preserve his honor in the eyes of society. But Mary would be publicly humiliated and probably executed by stoning.

The other choice was really to do nothing: say nothing to anyone, get Mary as far away as possible, resign himself to never seeing her again, then ride out the storm in silence.

Joseph was the perfect example of what the Old Testament calls a "just man." He acted on the basis of his values, on his sense of righteousness, rather than on his grasp of the circumstances. He didn't pull back from this disruption of his life. He faced it, he plunged into it, even if he had no idea where that plunge would land him.

It is intriguing to see that it is only after Joseph had struggled his way through this reflection and decision, that he was given a share in God's own understanding, and began to realize just how truly new his life was to be . . . that what seemed to be human weakness, betrayal and infidelity, was in fact the hand of God re-shaping his life, reshaping the world. Joseph could have wal-lowed in self-pity and bitterness, and no one would have blamed him. But he didn't. He chose rather to open himself up to a loving relationship he couldn't possibly understand or predict, a future he would never have chosen for himself.

Joseph, too, must color our life-long Advent wait for the com-ing of Christ. He teaches us to be sure that we do not become so taken up with our own design that we do not notice it when Christ comes into our lives in his own way, on his own terms. He teaches us to be aware of and not to fear the fact that the reality of the Incarnation, if we see it as it is, will make demands of us, will make changes in our lives, our plans, our expectations of our-selves and of one another.

So to the hope of Isaiah, the trust of Mary, and the fervor of John we add on this last Sunday of Advent the courage of Joseph. His too is an Advent virtue. And it must be ours.

Christmas

God has chosen to dwell with his people. He has chosen to be Emmanuel, which means "God with us." As a sign a virgin has conceived and borne a Son who is the Almighty, the Counsellor, the Prince of Peace.

And in this one event, in time 2,000 years ago, in Bethlehem, the first great era of human history was brought to a close, and the course was set for the future of all creation. God had chosen to dwell with his people because earlier, much earlier, his people had chosen not to dwell with God. In the imagery of the book of Genesis we are told that in the beginning we were one with God, we were his people indeed. But then, as now, the choice was free, and mankind chose to change all that. Unity with God and among people was destroyed. But with this fall there came the promise, the promise that humankind would one day again be made whole. So there began the years of formation. God began again to create for himself a people. Through many years and many stages, through all the covenants of the Old Testament with Abraham, with Joseph, with Moses, with David, with Solomon, the promise and the call were the same: "I will be your God, and you will be my people."

Finally humankind had been brought again to the point at which it was able to respond with a total "Yes" in the person of Mary. And with that "Yes" we were once again ready to be given the gift of fidelity, ready to be made capable of living as God's people at one with him.

But if this event, this taking of human flesh, was the close of one era, it was the beginning of another. The era in which we live out our Christianity, the era of God present with his people, present in human form, human acts, human abilities. The Incarnation, once begun, has never ceased, and never will. God's choice to take on human nature, human flesh and blood and mind and feeling is as real and immediate now as it was in Bethlehem. The humanity Christ claims today is ours. The flesh and blood, the hearts and minds he claims as his are our own.

So in a very real sense God's people must not only celebrate the Incarnation, God's people must be the Incarnation. We must, each of us, be Christ Incarnate, Christ in the flesh, for every other human being. Those whom we will meet today, tomorrow, at home, at work, on the street, depend on us to make Christ real, to give him human form and human life.

Holy Family

Certainly the fact that Christ grew up in a family setting was more than simply an historical accident. Christ could, I suppose, have chosen any number of ways of moving in to the human scene. But he chose to be shaped as any human being is shaped. He chose to be, as St. Paul puts it, literally "like us" in every detail. It is simply true to say that in a very real sense Christ became the person he was because Joseph and Mary were the people they were. And that is a process he chose to undergo. That means that there is something about that process that is genuinely sacred, necessarily human, and that to have avoided it would have meant that Christ would have been something other than fully human.

The family atmosphere, the family influence, is the deepest and most formative element in a person's life. That is most true, of course, of one's original family, the family in which one grew up. Almost everything that a child does is in one way or another an imitation of his or her parents or older brothers and sisters. Almost every habit, every attitude that is acquired, is in some way a reflection, either positively or negatively, of the effect that other family members have had.

It is in intimate companionship with other people, and only that way, that one becomes human, or at least what God means by human. And that is true at any age, in any setting: childhood, youth, adulthood, old age, a nuclear family, an extended family, a small group who shares similar interests, or a large community with many interests. It is by such intimate interaction that a person

11

learns to be sensitive to the presence, the needs, the rights of other human beings. It is only in such interaction that a person comes to see oneself as an individual with one's own rights and one's own responsibilities. Simply enough, it is in such interaction that a person learns to love.

So to promote, to encourage in one another the ability to love creatively and responsibly, is the first and most basic task of any gathering of human beings, anywhere. That is what family means. All the rest, the house, the clothes, the food, the work, the play, all of those are just not good enough if that first is not successful.

Let us treasure very carefully our family life. It is a valuable thing. It is meant, by God's design, to provide us with powers we desperately need. But like so many valuable things, it is fragile. It can be weakened, even destroyed, by thoughtlessness, insensitivity. To avoid that requires patient, loving effort. But it is worth it. It works. It saves. Christ spent thirty years of his life doing just that. And that, every bit as much as his next three years, brought salvation. The Holy Family was no accident. Neither must be ours.

Mary, the Mother of God

In some ways, I suppose, New Year's is the most hectic time of the holiday season. There is always a lot of frantic celebrating that is as often as not done more out of a sense of duty than out of any real feeling of expectant joy at the prospect of a new year. But really, I suppose, celebration is appropriate for New Year's. New beginnings are always kind of joyful things.

So there is a certain freshness to the day, a readiness to believe that we are not, in fact, slaves to the past, that we can renew our lives, refresh our efforts to make of ourselves the kind of people we want to be, that we know we should be. I think it is just a part of human nature, this readiness to believe that somehow the new year will be better.

I say it is a part of human nature, and it is. But, more importantly, I think it is a part of divine nature as well. This eagerness to grow, to perfect ourselves and our world, is a grace, it is a gift, the gift of hope. New Year's Day is really a celebration of hope. And what a profoundly Christian virtue hope is. It is Christ who gives substance to our hope. It is our faith in the fact that God has united himself to our human efforts, so that all of the barriers, all of the limits to what human beings can make of themselves, have been removed, that is what makes our hope something more than idle dreaming. We are absolutely justified, because of Christ, in hoping for the best from the New Year, the best from ourselves in the New Year. We are justified in hoping for peace in a war-torn world, for charity in a world that tolerates and in many ways even seems to encourage the victimization of the weak and the poor. Perhaps that is really the best understanding of the virtue of hope, a willingness to suspend our critical judgment of the world, a willingness to judge the goodness of the world and of people not so much on the basis of what seems to be true to our senses but rather on the basis of what we know to be true in our hearts and minds. Hope springs from a willingness to judge the world as God judges it. Certainly that was the insight of the shepherds and Magi at Bethlehem, the insight even of Joseph and Mary themselves. Their surroundings, the evidence of their senses, wouldn't lead them to expect much from that event. But their faith led them to expect a great deal. And they did. The birth of Christ became for them a font of great hope, a hope that was fulfilled.

Epiphany

I suppose that in all of Scriptures there aren't very many symbols that show a deeper insight into human nature than the story of the Magi who set out to find the Christ child. The three wise men are all of humanity, really, a humanity constantly, restlessly in search of God.

From the very beginning that has been the human quest. As human beings we have never really been content with our own company, our own limitations. One of the threads that ties together the mythology, the legends, of virtually every culture in the world is that somehow the heroes managed to leave behind the company of ordinary human beings, and move in the company of immortals.

But the story of the Magi, the story of Epiphany, differs from the story of any other search for God ever made. These exotic, wealthy, intellectual, mystical men, men with every tool at their disposal, were unable to end their search, unable to find God, until they had plunged themselves totally, openly, and trustingly into the most ordinary circumstances imaginable: a barn, providing a few nights shelter for some animals, a peasant girl, a new baby, and a very confused husband.

With the journey of the Magi, humankind's search for God took on a totally new and unexpected shape. No more could that search be made by leaving humanity and its concerns behind. From then on God would reveal himself through the efforts, the cares, the needs of human beings. The face of God was no further away than the face of the nearest person. The birth of Christ and the discovery of the Magi cleared away what Isaiah in the first reading called "the thick cloud that till now has covered the people." Now, because of Christ, every human being, each of us, is revealed as we really are: a divine idea, an immortal creature.

But if we are to find God in the lives of other people, that means that others must be able to find God in us. Our lives are the instruments that God has chosen for his Epiphany, the showing forth of his presence. If we make of those lives less than the best of which we are capable, then we end up playing the role of Herod. We become the obstacles to the search. We are the ones who de-rail and deceive those who seek for God. We must live out, honestly and completely, whatever our state in life may be. Whatever our physical and emotional and mental equipment, whatever our assets and liabilities, we must use them to the fullest. What may be the role that is given to us, demanded of us, in life and the talents we may or may not have in playing it out is not really very important. But the sincerity, the honesty with which we accept this role, and conscientiously play it out as God's own Epiphany—that is infinitely important.

Baptism of the Lord

The liturgical readings shift focus now, and we are confronted with the image not of a child but of a full grown man. The revelation now is not so much who is this person but rather what has he come to do.

More than likely, in the mind of Isaiah the imagery of the servant of God was meant to apply not so much to any one particular person but rather to all of Israel. But the Gospel authors change that. In the baptism narrative each of them takes that image and applies it to the person of Christ. It is he in whom the Father is well pleased and on whom his Spirit rests. Everything that had been promised in Isaiah's prophecy, Christ would take upon himself to do.

And so he did. Christ chose to save the world, to institute the New Kingdom, not by calling on the power and majesty of God's Son, but rather by confronting the world with the gentleness of Isaiah's servant, by saying to the world and everyone in it for the first time, "I won't hurt you. I want nothing for you but your own good." And he pursued that good with all of the tools and skills of gentleness. Tools and skills like fidelity, patience, and faithfulness. A willingness to wait patiently and calmly, without fear or anger, when it seemed that very little was going the way he might have wished. Christ, after all, during his own lifetime saw very little progress made in what he came to do. For every follower he gained, he made a couple of enemies. And while his followers were among the poor and the weak, his enemies were usually among the rich and the powerful.

Such was the baptism of Christ. A baptism into the role of the servant of God, a role of gentleness, of endurance, and of joyful confidence. And such certainly is our baptism as well. To what extent are our lives marked by that same gentleness? I think our baptism calls us to reflect very seriously on the violence that we heap on one another in so many ways . . . with words, for one. Gossip, criticism, ridicule. The violence of our attitudes, our values. Any attitude that really says to another in any way, "You just don't matter very much" or any attitude that allows us to sacrifice the peace of mind, the well-being of any other person in order to bolster our own sense of well-being, is violent.

So let us today, and as many times as it takes, renew our acceptance of our own baptism and our resolve to live it out as gently, as patiently, and as publicly as did Christ. And let us do so utterly confident that it works. In our baptism the Spirit has settled on us and the Father has told us, "What the Spirit will make of you pleases me." That is all that matters.

Second Sunday in Ordinary Time

The Gospel reading this weekend centers again on the compelling of John the Baptist. As usual, John had quite a crowd gathered about him, and when he saw Christ coming towards him John publicly acknowledged him as the Messiah and named himself as his witness.

That word is really quite a complex one. To be a witness means that a person has learned something. He has come into contact with a truth. He has seen it or heard it or been told of it.

But the witness is not just a learner. The witness is one who gives public testimony to the truth of what has been learned, and a third element is that the witness must do so persistently. And when that truth is opposed, as it often is from one source or another, his only real security is in his faithfulness, his persistence.

John's example teaches us something we need to know about what it means to give witness. I said that truth will always be opposed from one source or another, in one way or another. And that is true. The believer who is a true witness, who publicly gives evidence of the truth, will probably be subject to some degree of opposition, perhaps of ridicule . . . some degree of suffering. In some sense "witness" will always mean "martyr."

So perhaps it is time for each of us to begin, or begin again, with an honest examination of the quality of our own witness. Does our choice of Christianity, our decision to believe, in any way set us apart from the values and practices of the society around us? It should. Is our acceptance of Christ and his way obvious, clear, evident? Is there a clear difference between what we say and do, and what is said and done by those around us who do not believe? Are there clear prophetic voices being raised in our own community, in our own parish, in witness to the truth? Voices raised not in judgment of evil, by itself, that does no good at all, but rather voices raised, example given, in clear affirmation and practice of the good. True witness is rarely a matter of pointing out someone else's faults . . . rather it is a matter of practicing, insistently practicing, one's own virtue. Openly. Clearly. Obviously. Every day, for each of us, there are opportunities to witness, to testify to the fact that it is God's world, and we are called to live in it on his terms. Faith without witness is empty and hypocritical. At this Mass, when we echo John's words at the Communion, when we say, "This is the Lamb of God, who takes away the sins of the world," let us, each of us, privately add his further words from the last line of this Gospel: "And I am his witness."

Third Sunday in Ordinary Time

Even for Paul, it is simply part of the human experience that something which can seem to start off so well, so simply, can get so mixed up and complicated.

Paul had made great progress in his early preaching. He must have been a compelling preacher, an attractive figure. The problem was there were other compelling figures around who were also making great progress in their work of conversion. Peter was one. And a third disciple, a man named Apollos, was another. And as these three, and others, traveled about calling people to the Gospel, the new converts were beginning to pay their loyalty not so much to Christ as they were to the one who had converted them.

And so in his letter to the people of Corinth Paul condemns that fractioning of the Church. He tells them that they have lost sight of the original value taught to them from the beginning, the Lordship of Christ, and him alone. Paul begs the people to settle their differences, regain, repurify their original vision, and get back to basics, simply enough, the love of Christians for Christ, and for one another.

He calls them to quick reform, to purge away all of the added issues, all of the concerns that may seem to be so important but in fact are just so much baggage that weighs them down in their pursuit of the truth. And a bit later in the same letter Paul reminds the people of the constant need for a careful, reflective vigilance in all of this. Values have a way of becoming lost in the shuffle, vision has a way of becoming clouded again and again.

And that means that those who would pursue the truth must be ready and willing to start over, to repurify, resimplify again and again, as often as is needed.

So many times in Scripture the call to reform seems to be presented as something that would be done once and for all and, once done, it would never be undone. The people of the early Church expected the coming of the Kingdom, which Christ promises in the Gospel, as something that would happen very soon in their own lifetime. It just didn't occur to them that one of the central virtues in their reform would simply be patience.

Well, 2,000 years later, we have a different perspective. That final fullness is not yet here. The Kingdom has grown, certainly, but it is far from complete. Patience and persistence are most definitely reform virtues.

I suppose there will always be a tension in the life of a believer between the picture drawn by Christ of what should be and our own experience of what is. A tension between Christ's clear and simple vision of the Kingdom and our own confused and muddied perception of our lives. And that tension will be for us a constant call to reform, to simplify, to purify.

Fourth Sunday in Ordinary Time

Reform is never a simple process. Sometimes it is outright painful. Certainly each period of reform in the history of the Church has been costly in terms of membership.

It has happened many times in our 2,000 year history, this cycle of growth and reform. Many times the Church has been rebuilt on a few, on what the prophet Zephaniah calls in the first reading a faithful remnant. And it will happen many times again.

And each time it has, or will yet, the spark has always been the same. Someone has taken seriously this Gospel reading for today, the Beatitudes, the values upon which the new Kingdom will be built. To those who see only with the eyes of the world, these Beatitudes are absurd. They certainly are not the values urged on us by our society, and anyone who follows them wholeheartedly runs a real risk of looking ridiculous in the eyes of the world. There is nothing at all in this reading that guarantees us comfort, popularity, the respect of our peers, success, position, and so on.

We are to be poor in spirit. That means that we should be satisfied and grateful if we are comfortable and well off, and satisfied and grateful if we are not.

Happy are the gentle, the peacemakers. Now, this says nothing at all about the morality of self-defense or the even the morality of a just war. But it does mean that a Christian refuses to see life as a battle, a contest, refuses to see any exchange between human beings in terms of who wins and who loses.

Happy are those who can mourn well and creatively. Those who can accept, even welcome, the pains and disappointments of life, those who recognize that as being as much and as creative a part of human living as are its joys.

Happy are the pure in heart, the singleminded, those who hunger and thirst for what is right, those who are even persecuted in the cause of righteousness. Those who are more concerned with whether or not a thing is right than with whether or not it is profitable, popular.

Happy are the merciful, the forgiving, those who refuse to keep scorecards on their friends, neighbors, enemies, those who refuse to replay over and over in their minds old hurts, offenses, insults. Those who refuse to surrender their ownership of the present to past hurt.

These are Christian values. The struggle to become like that is what it means to be Christian. They are, most often, not the values of the world into which Christ sends us. And so it is in that struggle that the reform to which Christ calls us is accomplished in the Church, in the world, and in ourselves.

Fifth Sunday in Ordinary Time

In this Gospel reading, Christ is pictured as giving his disciples the first in a series of instructions. In language that is clear and simple and direct, he tells them just what they are to do, how they are to act.

And Christ begins these instructions by setting up for his disciples two images: the image of salt and the image of light.

Salt preserves. It maintains health and strength. But even more than that it enhances, it makes things better. It brings out the true flavor, the true goodness of whatever it seasons.

And light. A lamp does no good for anyone if you light it and then cover it up with a basket. In fact, a lamp really isn't a light at all if it isn't out in the open where people can see it and benefit from the fact that it shows the way.

Today it is we who are the disciples to whom Christ gives these instructions. It is we who take these images to heart and be for the world salt and light. We must season one another, bring out the goodness in one another.

In any relationship in any setting, at work, at recreation, at school, in casual contacts, our role is the same . . . to preserve, to strengthen, to encourage goodness, to enlighten, to dispel darkness and shadows. That is what salt and light do. And we are to be the salt and light of the earth.

To the world ours can seem a religion of extremes. Extreme enough to believe that God became human and that in us there is now to be found divine goodness. Extreme enough to insist that simple, weak human beings can indeed love their enemies, do good to those who hurt them, to insist that human beings can indeed live as they have been created, in the image and likeness of God, and that to do so is a value greater than any other imaginable, greater than wealth, power, fame, popularity, comfort, anything.

Well, how do we do that? We can never hope to rationally convince anyone of the rightness of our way of life. We can only show them. And in the last line of the Gospel, he explains what that must mean. Stand out before people, so that everyone can see goodness in your acts.

So the message, then, is simply that. We season creation and we light the way to goodness by living out that goodness. The extent to which we center our lives around values, around what is right, and act on that, simply because it is right, quite apart from whether or not it is comfortable, fun, profitable or popular, to that extent we will truly be the salt of the earth. We will season those whom we touch, and we will invite others to respond in the same way, with the goodness that is in them.

First Sunday of Lent

The Gospel, like the first reading this weekend, is a story of temptation, the temptation of Christ himself. Matthew's account is a series of invitations that Satan offers to Christ to set aside the slow painful limitations of his human nature and to use his power as the Son of God to get his job done quickly and effortlessly, to solve his problems with no personal involvement, no personal commitment, no personal sacrifice. "Turn the stones into bread. Jump off the tower of the Temple, and when you land unharmed, everyone will follow you. One world, one people, united under you. Pay homage to me, and I will give you the whole world, uncontested. You could be a wise and benevolent ruler, assuring peace and prosperity for everyone." Sounds good. To feed the hungry, to be recognized as God's own, as the Messiah, to bring peace and prosperity to the world, those were all things Christ would have badly wanted to accomplish. It would have been so easy for him to have said "Yes."

Ultimately, of course, it wouldn't have worked. Satan's temptations were lies. They always are. If Christ had based his Kingdom only on power, it would soon have crumbled. It would not have been the Kingdom intended by the Father, a nation of free believers, who freely choose to live out their lives not just for present satisfaction, but in preparation for an infinite future.

So Christ recognized these "opportunities" for what they were. Temptations. Lies. Impossible fantasies that would actually be the undoing of everything he had hoped to accomplish.

Each one of us, perhaps many times in the course of our lives, face such temptations. We too must decide. Are we going to commit ourselves to a process of real growth in the real world, a mixture of success and failure, happiness and pain, companionship and loneliness, the company of good and wise people, certainly, but that of the weak and foolish as well? Or are we going to give into the temptations, the thousand and one invitations we get every day to flee from the real world, to pretend that it is something it is not? The temptation to avoid responsibility, the temptation to avoid involvement in other people's lives and other people's needs.

It is not by accident that we hear these readings on the first Sunday of Lent. Sooner or later we will each of us find ourselves in the wilderness, spiritually and emotionally. Any number of paths out will be offered. Most of them will be lies. And what we have built of discipline in our lives will be our only assurance of success.

Second Sunday of Lent

I'm sure that everyone of us has at one time or another had the experience of being struck with the fact that, at the heart of it all, things are really developing about as they should. It is as though the lid were being lifted off of daily life for just a moment, and we see a hint of the real dynamics, the real value of those lives.

These moments bring into our lives a great gift, the gift of confidence in the present.

Christians usually find it easy to be confident about the past. It is a simple matter to see the hand of God at work when we look back. We can see how over the centuries, humankind has moved from a sort of fearful awe of natural powers, to a parent and child relationship with a personal God.

For a Christian it is relatively easy to be confident about the future. Over and over again we are reminded of Christ's promise to return to human society, to take up his own personal rule over a new Kingdom.

But for a lot of people, even for believers, it seems to be a very difficult thing to work up any real trust in the present. From a steady stream of talk shows and public opinion polls, and just casual conversation, it is pretty easy to conclude that most of us probably fear, if not outright believe, that the forces for change that are at work around us right now are largely destructive ones.

Well, the Gospel reading for today speaks to that, I think. The fact is that the constructive hand of God is as much at work in the forces that are shaping our experience today as it was when the apostles were granted a glimpse beneath the surface, in the Transfiguration, and they saw the Son of God moving in the midst of his people.

And that is the truth of the Transfiguration. Even when hidden Christ is fully and divinely at work in our lives in the ideas, the feelings, the people that affect, change, and transform those lives.

And that means that people as ordinary as you and I can bring to bear on their challenges and problems not only their own efforts and abilities but those of Christ as well. We can never know the full result of our efforts because we can never know the full extent of the powers that are being poured into those efforts through us.

And I think that adds a dimension of depth to our Lenten reflections. It is a great self-discipline indeed to confidently face one's fears and hesitancy, to not trust them. To place one's trust instead in that basic sense of rightness, that sacred insight that "This is how my life should be, even if it doesn't feel right for a while." There is a tremendous power of Transfiguration in such a stance.

Third Sunday of Lent

This Gospel reading we have just heard is one of the longest, richest, and most complex readings to which we are exposed during the course of the liturgical year. As Christ is traveling toward Jerusalem he passed through a Samaritan town and stopped at a well to get a drink of water. While he is sitting there he strikes up a conversation with a woman from the town who had also come by to draw water.

It is Christ who directs this conversation from the very beginning. From a hostile beginning the woman very quickly becomes a listener, then a believer, then a witness to what she believes.

One of John's favorite devices in presenting the teaching of Christ is the almost constant misunderstanding of those who listen to him.

Christ speaks to the woman of a living water, a water that will never stop flowing, that can be hers for the asking. But she is rooted in the immediacy of her own experience. She has a hard time lifting her vision beyond the here-and-now needs of hunger and thirst, day-to-day survival. She says, "That sounds pretty good. Give me some of that. I won't ever have to come back to this well."

But then Christ very abruptly adds a new dimension to the conversation, almost a surprising one. He says, "Go home and get your husband." She says, "I don't have one." And Christ's response is very pointed. He says, "That's right, you don't. The man you are living with now is not your husband." That hits pretty close to home, so the woman pulls back from that encounter. She quickly changes the subject.

So the message is clear. Before any of the other prayers that the woman might choose to make could be effective, before any of the promises made by Christ, the bread of life, the living water, a sense of fulfillment and satisfaction, a sense of rightness about one's life, before any of that could take root in her, there was something that had to be done first, another act had to be placed . . . to use the word that we've been using for the past month or so, an act of reform.

And the same thing, really, can be said of any weakness, any failure, any sin in our lives. If there is for us, as there was for the Samaritan woman, a thirst, an emptiness, a weariness in our lives, it is so because there is something at home, something inside of us, where we live, that is not right. Exactly like the woman in the Gospel, before we can come to Christ and hope to be satisfied, we must first follow his direction to go home, turn to the center of our lives, face what is wrong there, and reform it.

Fourth Sunday of Lent

This Gospel reading is one of the relatively few incidents that is recorded in each of the four Gospels. But where Matthew, Mark, and Luke report the event, and incorporate it into the whole of their Gospels, John translates it. He translates it into images. Two images, really, to which the incident, the healing of a blind man, lends itself very well. The images of darkness and of light.

The darkness of the man born blind is really just a symbol of the darkness that can, at times, surround us, into which we can stumble. And the light of the new vision given him is, for us, a symbol of the light that can change or renew our world.

And the light does indeed make us new. When the man came back from the pool of Siloam, when he had moved out of the darkness and into the light, some of his neighbors didn't recognize him. The light changes our lives. It changes us. We are not the same once we have moved into the truth, the light. Old patterns, old attitudes, old ways of relating to those around us change. They just aren't good enough anymore.

The Pharisees, those who had an investment in the darkness, began to question the man, question him challengingly. He was different now, and that made him a threat. They ask him, "What happened?" He answers, "I don't know." "Who did this?" "I don't know, who he is." "Where is he?" "I don't know." "What is so special about him? What gives him the right to upset people's lives?" "I don't know that either."

In fact, all that the man knew was that the light was good. His life was better than it had been. This exchange between the man and the Pharisees is a beautifully crafted passage. In effect, the Pharisees are trying to convince him that what had happened to him really wasn't good, that he should be leery, suspicious of it, even reject it. And it would have been easy, really, for him to have agreed with them. But he didn't. He couldn't give a coherent, convincing defense of what had happened. He didn't even try. Nor did he ask anyone else to do so. Not even his parents. He simply knew that whatever had happened, it was good. He didn't try to strip his movement of mystery and risk. He simply focused on the fact that the darkness was bad, and whatever had happened it wasn't the darkness, so it must be better. For him, Christ didn't need to be explained or defended. He only needed to be trusted.

And so he did. He got up, went to the pool, went to where the newness was to be found, and embraced it. And because he did, his life was changed. He was freed from what had been, and he began to live in the light.

Fifth Sunday of Lent

One of the things about this Gospel reading that strikes me each time I go through it is how many times the people involved, even the apostles, even Christ's close friends, Martha and Mary, tried to tell Christ he was going about all of this all wrong.

At the outset, Martha and Mary invite Christ to come visit Lazarus, who is sick. But Christ doesn't go. He waits two days more. Then he says to the apostles, "O.K., let's go now." But they object. They say it is too dangerous a trip to make. Christ says, "Lazarus needs me." They answer, "No, he doesn't. He'll get better on his own." Finally Christ tells them, "He's already dead. Now let's go." Interestingly enough it is Thomas, the doubter, who is the first to say to the others, "Well, we'll probably all be killed, but O.K., let's go."

And when Jesus arrives at Bethany the first thing he hears is somebody else telling him he hadn't handled the whole thing very well. Martha says, "You are late. You should have come sooner." In effect she tells him, "If you had done it my way, it would have worked out all right."

At the tomb they are joined by Mary, and the first thing she says is the same old line. "Where were you? If you had acted like a Messiah is supposed to act, you could have prevented all this."

By that time, the chorus had been pretty well taken up by the whole crowd. If he could cure a blind man he should have been able to prevent this. And so, again "troubled in spirit," the Gospel says Jesus asks some of the men to move away the stone that sealed the door of the tomb. And again, Martha tells him he is doing it wrong. This time her complaint is about the odor from a four-day old corpse.

And the outcome of it all, of course, was that the trip, which had seemed pointless, even foolishly dangerous to the apostles, the death and pain of separation that had seemed so burdensome to Martha and Mary, the confidence, the trust that had seemed so misplaced to the rest of the bystanders, all of this was seen to be very purposeful indeed. Once they stopped trying to write the script, and simply, honestly began to at least try to see their lives as God sees them, then everything that had been so bad became good. Lazarus was alive. Christ had not been too late. The apostles were in no danger from the crowds. The promise of life was kept, and the faith of Christ's friends, their love for him, grew stronger.

In a life lived on God's terms, there is no tragedy, none that lasts. What Christ said to Lazarus as he opened his tomb, he says to each of us, to all of his people, "Untie them. Let them go free."

Passion (Palm) Sunday

The reading of the Passion this morning is from the Gospel of Matthew. The imagery is simple and brutal. It is that of a human being taunted and tortured by other human beings, that of great suffering which human beings choose to inflict on others.

But this time the victim of human cruelty was so much more than human. Christ was the Son of God. The Creator of all that is good in human nature freely took on himself all that is evil in that nature. And that is the mystery. Christ did not have to suffer. He chose to. He was not overpowered by human cruelty, rather he submitted himself to it. On the cross, he was not simply victim, he was priest as well.

Christ could have chosen any other course. But he chose that course, and he had done so centuries before the time of Calvary. It is as though the Crucifixion were really only one in a series of events that had been set in motion at the very beginning. The first time that God looked at humankind, and chose what he saw, not simply as more of his creatures, but as his people, the people with whom he would remain no matter what, it was as though the Crucifixion had already begun. And had he chosen otherwise, had he chosen not to be the priest-victim, not to endure the worst that his creatures could do to him, then he would have still been God, but we would not have been his people.

Well, why? What is there about the bond, the relationship between God and humanity that can twist the patience and faithfulness of Christ into a sentence of death. And again, Matthew's

37

answer is simple and direct. It is sin. Christ's faithfulness led to Calvary, because he was alone in that faithfulness. The evil of sin, then is seen not only in the torture that Christ endured, but in the fact that he endured it alone. It is the abandonment of Christ, the faithlessness of even those who professed to follow him, those followers who simply became "the crowd," that is, the true revelation of the sin of humankind.

Lent will, again, come to an end for us this week. I hope that this season has been for each of us truly a season of penance, of self-examination, of confronting the heartlessness, the dullness in our lives. Sin, once it is recognized and rejected, has lost its power over us. We are not at all slaves to our past, to our habits, to our weakness. We are God's people, and we have a share in everything that is his. And just as surely as we have again and again taken part in his crucifixion, so shall we always, as often as we choose to do so, take part in his rising again.

Easter

Jesus Christ, the Son of God, who died and was buried, has risen from the dead. And in his resurrection all of us, all humankind, all of creation is made new. Again tonight the Easter story has been told. The followers of Christ who saw him die and mourned his death returned in the early hours of the morning to where he had been buried, and they found an empty tomb. And there they heard the words of God's messenger, "He is not here. He is risen. Look for him among the living."

And for two thousand years those same joyful words, "He is risen," have echoed from a million other tombs. Hatred, greed, violence, fear, all of the tombs in which we bury ourselves and one another have been broken open. They have no power to hold anyone. These tombs too are just so many empty shells.

And again tonight God's word is sent to us, as it was to Mary Magdalene, "Do not be afraid." And it is true, we have nothing to fear. God became like us. He lived a human life. He did the things we do, he felt the things we feel. He took upon himself the wages of all human sin and human failure. He took upon himself the worst that human beings can do to one another. He suffered the effects of human weakness, greed, violence, and hatred. And finally he took upon himself the ultimate violence, the ultimate human absurdity, death itself. But this tomb too he left empty, so that with what St. Paul would later call the great foolishness of Christianity, we can say that even death has lost its terror. All of life has been made new. Everything that happens to us has been revealed in a new light. And we can see clearly now that there is no challenge so great that it cannot be met, no burden so heavy that it cannot be borne. We are all of us again tonight called to take up a share in the risen life of Christ.

In the Gospels the glorified risen body of Christ was not a wispy spiritual thing that had somehow been drawn out of the stream of human experience. Rather the glorified body of Christ was very much a thing of flesh and blood, a thing that clearly bore, as Thomas was to learn, the marks of Christ's involvement with the challenges of living.

The mark of our resurrection, then, of our baptism, is not how little involved we become, how far away we manage to remain from the daily tombs of human living, but rather how fearlessly and joyfully we enter them. This is not only the day that the Lord has made, this is the world that the Lord has made, the world which he brought with him out of the tomb. Indeed, let us be glad and rejoice in it.

Second Sunday of Easter

Over these past few weeks we have taken long and prayerful looks at the core of historical events from which our Creed springs. Christ, who was a real human being, lived in a real place, at a real time, died a real death, and was buried in a real grave.

But because he was also the Son of God, he rose from the dead, and again lived, a real human being in a real place at a real time. No one makes that point more clearly than does Thomas in the Gospel reading for today. His appearance to the apostles could not be dismissed as wishful thinking or the fruit of an over-active imagination.

But far beyond the bare facts we have given thought, too, to what they mean. Because God himself confronted and experienced human weakness and suffering and death and overcame them, those things can never again be experienced in quite the same way by any human being. God cannot act foolishly, meaninglessly. So if God suffered and died there must be sense and meaning to suffering and death. They no longer mean the end of happiness and joy nor even the end of life itself.

Now that is a lot to try to think about in a few days. Christianity is not a simple thing. It is as complex as human nature, and as mysterious as divine nature. Christianity seems to demand of us an almost more than human ability to practice any number of virtues. Patience, optimism, persistence, forgiveness, charity. And Christianity even demands of us that we practice these virtues in situations in which to do so may very well seem inappropriate, frustrating, even foolish. If all we have to go on is our experience of the world, we can cast about for some time and not come up with too terribly many good reasons for being patient, optimistic, persistent, forgiving, and charitable. Somehow, if these virtues are going to be practiced with any integrity, we must be made able to know more about the world and our life in it than we are able to draw simply from our immediate experience.

And that is really just a complicated way of saying that a Christian, before anything else, must be a believer. Faith ties together all of the complex elements of our Christianity, simplifies them, into one challenge. To accept the fact that it is God's world, that he has visited and changed it to suit his purpose. And because of that, human experience can never be a very reliable yardstick to use in judging good and evil, truth and error. Only God's word can possibly be such a yardstick in his world.

And if we apply that yardstick faithfully then all of the other virtues will flow through our lives much more naturally and easily. As St. Peter writes in the second reading this morning, "Protect your faith. Treasure it. There is cause for rejoicing there."

Third Sunday of Easter

One of the most common scriptural images that is used to represent all of life, really, but most particularly the spiritual life, the life of grace, is the image of a journey. And it is an appropriate one, really. To go on a journey means to make a move. It means to leave something behind and set out for something else . . . something that may be unfamiliar, may be uncertain, may even be frightening. But the only way to get there, the only way to eliminate the uncertainty and the fear, is to make the move.

And that should be a familiar image, really. We are so often called to move out, to change our attitudes, our values, our ideas. That, after all, is what it means to grow. And just as a journey that is not marked by movement can never be successful, so neither can a life that is not marked by growth. Truly, in every dimension of our lives, we have only two choices. Either we grow or something in us dies.

In the Gospel those travelers on the road to Emmaus must have been two very sad, disillusioned men. And then, as they go along, they are joined by a stranger. Naturally enough they begin to talk to him about what is on their mind. At first it seems as though the conversation just isn't going anywhere. It seems as though the stranger doesn't understand them, nothing he says helps all that much.

But finally, little by little, conversation becomes communication, and if nothing else, they become interested. And it is really at this point, as they end their physical journey, that they begin their spiritual, emotional journey. They begin to go through the painful process of leaving behind an old misunderstanding and opening themselves to the newness of truth. I say they begin here. And begin is all that it is. They were interested, they were willing to talk a little bit about growth. But talk is all, so far.

But finally the moment comes, as it inevitably does, when they are confronted with reality of Christ present in our lives and the true nature of his mission. They did, the reading says, recognize him.

We, too, are travelers, just as were the two in the Gospel. And so many times we, too, make that journey full of plans and expectations that don't work out. We, too, are sometimes disappointed, disillusioned on our journey. But just as they were we, too, are called to recognize the companionship of Christ on the journey and to realize that in the light of that companionship our own misdirections and misunderstandings don't really mean very much. No journey made in the company of Christ can ever possibly be a failure, even if we end up far from where we expected to be when we set out. As long as we end up where he calls us to be the journey is worthwhile.

Fourth Sunday of Easter

This Gospel passage underscores for me what a fragile thing, how easily threatened, our sense of identity is as separate individual human beings, our sense of who we are, what we are, why we are.

So much of our contact with the institutions of society has been structured in such a way as to be very dehumanizing, depersonalizing. Just look through your wallet, or purse, or desk drawer sometime. Thumb through all of the cards and pieces of paper that describe you as a number. Try to trace your records through a bank, a courthouse, a hospital, the Internal Revenue Service. So many times there isn't much more than a computer file to show that a human being has passed through those institutions, experienced them, perhaps experienced them movingly, intensely, profoundly.

Well, to me this kind of reflection gives great impact to the image that Christ draws of himself in this Gospel reading today, the image of a shepherd that knows his sheep and calls each of them by name. In all of God's people there is no such thing as a faceless, nameless number. We are, after all, what God has made us to be, uniquely valuable individuals, individual enough to be known and recognized by Christ as a person apart from any other person and valuable enough to be loved by him.

Now that is a staggering thought when it really sinks in. We are, each one of us, completely known to Christ. Just think for a moment of all the things about yourself that you like. All the virtues, the strengths, the temptations resisted, the challenges met, the good deeds done that somehow seem to got unnoticed and unrespected by the people around you.

And then think about all of the things about ourselves that we try very hard to keep hidden from the people around us: the weaknesses, the fears, the vices that are really more embarrassing than evil. The sort of qualities that we fear would make us a good deal less loved, less respected, if they were known.

Well, they are known. All of the virtue in each of us is seen and known, and named, by Christ. The world may not notice nor be much impressed by our personal struggles to be virtuous. But that really doesn't matter. Christ does.

And the weakness too. The great truth is that Christ loves and calls by name weak and foolish and fearful people. Christ has no disdain or contempt for our faults. He knows human beings too well for that. He calls us away from those faults, certainly. He encourages, leads, and shepherds us away from them. But even that is a gentle and loving process. There is, finally, only one measure of what we are, any of us, and that is the great truth that Christ calls each of us by name.

Fifth Sunday of Easter

I doubt that there is any more inspired or inspiring passage in all of Scripture than that section of the Gospel of John that begins the reading for today.

For the other Gospel writers in many places it seems to be their intention to present Christ as very much a human being, walking and talking and eating and sleeping and praying just as does anyone else. And of course that is true. But John seems to have been particularly struck by the fact that it was only part of the truth. John emphasized the majesty, the transcendence of the Christ-God, and he tries to call out of his readers a response that at least begins to be proportionate to that majesty. He tells us that we are so much more than we could ever imagine ourselves to be. He invests every smallest detail of our human lives with an importance, a dignity that is truly infinite in its scope.

Thomas and Philip, like the others, must have been pretty stunned, and upset by the news that Christ was about to leave them. So one of them sort of stammers out, "Well, what about us? What are we supposed to do now?" And Christ answers, in effect, "You know very well what you are supposed to do. You have been watching me for three years. Do what I have done." And then he adds a few lines later, "I assure you, if you have faith in me, you will be able to do the things I have done, and far greater things."

Just reflect on that line for a moment. Every life, motivated by faith, no matter how humbly, even fruitlessly spent in the eyes of the world, is a gift offered to God, a sacrifice which draws all of humankind closer to salvation. In Christ's design the contribution to the salvation of the world that can be made by the keenest mind, the most dedicated activist, the most eloquent prophet, is really no greater, no more valuable, than that which can be made by the simplest, the least important, the least influential among us.

So there are no meaningless lives, there are no meaningless acts. There are only people who refuse to give meaning to their lives, their acts, or better, who refuse to recognize the meaning God has given to them. We cannot place our faith in the goodness of God, the goodness of his world, the creative power of his Word, somewhere off in an indefinable future. That faith must be placed in the world in which he has placed us, in that Word spoken to our own circumstances, no matter how they may seem to be. In his response to Philip's request to see the Father, Christ urges him to look beneath the surface of whatever, whoever is right in front of him. That is where the Father in all of his goodness and power has chosen to be.

Sixth Sunday of Easter

The first reading over these past few weeks has been a passage from the book of Acts. And they have pictured that kind of euphoria, that sense of having made it, having triumphed, that the early Church must have felt.

But this Gospel passage today begins to temper that sense of completeness, of having arrived at the end of the journey of faith. John wrote his Gospel perhaps some sixty years after the time of Christ. And over those years, he must have come to see that that sense of completeness, of triumph, had been just a little bit misplaced. From all that had happened, it was clear that God has chosen us. Now it must be made clear that we have chosen God.

So the long, sometimes painful, but always valuable process of reforming oneself from within, of bringing one's mind and heart into accord with the mind of God, is the process to which we are called by the saving power of Christ. But once called we are certainly not abandoned in this process. Rather Christ calls us to become personally involved in the process of our own salvation precisely because he himself is so intimately involved in the process of our salvation. If it is sometimes easy to say "No" to the call of faith it is never necessary to do so, no matter how difficult the situation may seem to be. Christ promises to send the Holy Spirit who will be for each of us the Spirit of truth, who will urge us from within to follow the way of truth. If we are open to the guidance of the Spirit, our choices will be Christ's own.

And there are two signs, I think, that can help tell us whether or not we are following the guidance of the Spirit. The Spirit calls us to the Church. We are invited as a people, and we must respond as such. If a choice we make, a way of life we build for ourselves, leads us further away from such communion, leads us to be influenced by, interact with fewer and fewer of God's people in worship, in learning, in the sacraments, then it is a bad choice, we are blocking out the movement of the Spirit.

And the Spirit urges us to a wholeness, an integrity, and the real satisfaction that such brings with it. Put more negatively, if we screw up our lives, if we are deaf to the call of the Spirit, then something in us hurts. If our lives are marked consistently by a dissatisfaction, a sense that something is wrong here, an emptiness, then that is a pretty good sign that we may be missing the direction in which the Spirit is trying to lead us. It is true that the life of grace may not always be easy or comfortable or pleasant. But followed honestly and persistently, it will feel right.

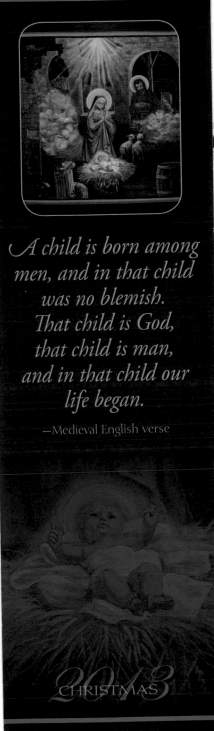

Ascension

sense of human passion and death in eadings. They are spoken with a calm, ken as if by one who knows indeed that nd earth has been given to him. There f uncertainty as to what will be the out- gives to his Church. The world will be leadership of Christ. The only question will happen, and how many will choose

been the case, certainly. For a number of perienced Christ as a man, very much in- from being covered in glory and able to rene certitude of divinity, Christ, in his in a very real way, as do we, on faith, on ct that God would somehow give mean- le up his life. The humanity of Christ is, ult thing for us to truly appreciate. We t in a very real sense Christ, during his view of his final glory than do we of our rist to the mount of the Ascension was nisgiving and insecurity as is our own. hose things in the only way a human Vith faith that God can see what we can- int to what seems pointless in our lives, here is. Christ was, after all, like us.

51

And if he was like us then that also means that we are like him. A life lived in trusting acceptance of the will of the Father led Christ to the glory of God, the fullness of perception and understanding. And so it will for us. That same glorious future is ours, if we are faithful. Just as with the Resurrection, the Ascension of Christ is both a revelation of himself and a promise made to all of his people. In another of his epistles St. Paul writes, "I consider the problems of this world as nothing compared to the glory that will be revealed in us."

So, the message of the Ascension is a simple one, really. Faithfulness works. Keep trying. Never quit. Christ's promises will be fulfilled and we, too, shall be covered with the glory of God.

Seventh Sunday of Easter

The feast of the Ascension, the readings for today, and those of next Sunday, the feast of Pentecost, really form one continuous narrative. And the narrative they form is sort of a Christmas story. This time not the birth of Christ but the birth of the Church.

For the apostles this time of waiting for a birth, like the first Advent, involved a good deal more than just waiting. It was a time of very active preparation, preparation to no longer simply be a follower but to, in their turn, begin to lead. To no longer simply stand in awe of the impact Christ had had on his society, now they must set out to have their own impact on many societies.

But there would be consequences for choosing to follow Christ. For the most part, those consequences would come in the form of the disapproval, the ridicule, the hatred of those around them. If they were going to find the strength to live out their choice of Christ's way, they were going to have to firmly root their new lives in the very source of that life, in God. They would have to give up the luxury of being approved by lots of other people and bring themselves to the point where they knew that being approved by God was good enough. And they did this in the only way possible. The last couple of lines in the first reading tell us how. They prayed.

Certainly it is true that today society's disapproval of Christian values doesn't take nearly as extreme a form as it did in the early Church. We don't face persecution. But we do face, if we openly choose Christ's way, being laughed at, ridiculed, ignored.

Christian values in a secular society can be difficult. And that means that those who would follow them honestly, today as with the apostles, must find within themselves the strength on which to rely, the strength to persevere, rather than rely on the acceptance and approval of those around us. And for us, as for the apostles, and for Mary, that means prayer. It means placing ourselves in the sort of situation in which the Father is the only important witness to our lives, the only one who truly can affirm those lives, truly judge our worth, our value. When we do that the choice of Christ's way becomes a good deal easier, regardless of consequences. There is no longer a need to be approved by the rest of the world. It becomes a natural thing to stand apart from society when it is wrong, even if that means incurring the judgment of that society.

Self-reliance, really, self-confidence. A dependence ultimately only on the judgment of the Father. That is part, at least, of the purpose of prayer. It has been since the beginning, and it is part of the rebirth of the Spirit we will celebrate on Pentecost.

Pentecost

Today we are celebrating the great and uniquely Christian mystery of Pentecost.

It begins with a picture of frightened people, people crippled, imprisoned by fear.

Fear of a very deadly sort, a kind of quiet dread that gnaws away at us. So quiet in fact that we may not even be able to give it a name. Far from prodding us to fight or run, this sort of fear does quite the opposite. It drags us down, ties weights to our hands and foot. It tells us, as it told the apostles, "Lock yourselves in your room. Find a corner and stay there. Don't try anything, because nothing you try is going to work out anyway. You don't have the ability, the strength, or even the charm to accomplish anything very valuable. Make no effort, take no risk, because if you do, you will fail."

The apostles, newly commissioned by Christ to go out to all the world as his witnesses, locked in a room, frightened of everything outside of that room. Frightened of persecution, certainly, but frightened too of ridicule, their own ignorance, the immenseness of their vocation, and the likelihood of their failure.

And had the event described for us in this first reading not happened, that would have been the history of all of humankind. But it did happen. Again, with the weakness of human nature, God merged the strength of his own divine nature. With the coming of the Holy Spirit, the apostles and all believers were given the ability to go beyond themselves, to draw on more than they ever thought they had.

55

We, too, have that Spirit of courage, that ability to go beyond ourselves. We are called, just as were the apostles, to a deep experience of the presence of the Spirit in our lives. We are called to let him work wonders through us. And he does. Everyone of us has had such an experience. Anytime we make an investment of ourselves in someone else's welfare, an investment of time or energy or talent or wealth, and do so really pretty certain that there will be no reward, perhaps not even any gratitude . . . any time we ask God for help, and keep on asking, even though there seems to be no help coming . . . anytime we say with confidence that God is indeed Lord of the world, that he gives it purpose and meaning, even though that can be pretty hard to see sometimes, anytime we make a real act of faith, just let ourselves go, completely, perhaps even desperately into God's hands, and experience that surrender as a victory, then we are truly caught up in the movement of the Spirit. We are going far beyond what human beings can do on their own. As the Gospel this morning tells us, God has indeed breathed on us, and we have been filled with the Holy Spirit.

Trinity Sunday

One of the forces over the long history of Revelation that gave shape and character to the Hebrew people was a strong sense of their own uniqueness. Unlike the religions that sprang up around the nature gods of other cultures, the worship of the Hebrews was a free response to a God who freely revealed himself, who drew close to his people. Slowly, really very slowly, over centuries, the people began to realize that at the heart of their uniqueness lay the fact that they didn't have to guess. They knew their God, and he knew them. One of the most fundamental credal formulas for the Hebrews was the phrase, "Our God is a God who speaks, who makes himself known."

And this revelation gave rise to something else new and unique. It fostered a quality of bond between God and his people that no other people had ever experienced . . . a relationship with God based on trust, confidence, truth, and strangest of all, on affection. The people were beginning to realize that their God was acting toward them and asking for their response in a way that could best be described as love.

So a God who spoke, who generated and sent out his word and, simply in the doing of that, gave rise to a third reality, a bond, a relationship because of that word. A bond of love.

But that tentative insight was only a beginning. It took the revealing presence of Christ to give fullness to the great mystery of the Trinity. Actually, even Christ's own human language fell short of this mystery. It was St. Augustine, really, who gave us the formula we use most commonly: Three Persons in one nature. Those words are a help, but they are not perfect. They don't truly lay open the mystery of the Trinity. Strictly speaking, we shouldn't really say that God is Three Persons in one nature. It would be more accurate to say that God is something like Three Persons in one nature.

But the inadequacy of language doesn't really matter. The truth is that the constant flow of life, of creative power, of love, that makes up the inner nature of God is not a closed circle. It has been broken open, and all of humankind has been included in it. We are not only God's creatures, we are his sons and daughters, we share in his own life. And that means that it is not only God's nature to know and to love creatively, it is our nature as well. If humankind is ever to become fully itself, fully what the Father intended it to be, then we must live out our likeness to God. We must become a true community, in which each member both creates and is created by the others, a community in which each member sees in others the perfection of God, so perfectly reflected that love is the only possible bond.

Corpus Christi

Today we celebrate the feast of the Body of Christ. And traditionally the focal point of this feast is two pronged. First, of course, a reaffirmation of our belief in the reality of Christ's presence in the Eucharist, physically, bodily. But also a time for reaffirming our belief in the fact that we are that Body as well. The Church, the People of God, bound together by a divine call. So really this feast is an appropriate setting in which to reflect on the quality of love, the life force of the Body of Christ, at its most radical, its most Christian.

And that is Christ's insistence that if we are to be truly his followers, we must love our enemies.

Just what is an enemy, really? There is a way, I think, to come to an appreciation of something at least of the impact of Christ's teaching to love one's enemies. Think of someone whom you know doesn't like you. Make it a real person, maybe more than one. Someone whom you know thinks you are a real jerk and who doesn't hesitate in the least to say so any chance that comes along. Someone who perhaps has even done you some real damage and is pretty likely to do so again in the future.

And then try to become aware of the sort of feelings that that image conjures up in you. Anger, perhaps resentment, inferiority, jealousy, fear, the painfully corrosive suspicion that just maybe that person is, after all, right.

And when your awareness of those feelings is clear, then just put them aside. Resolve not to use those feelings, not to let them dictate the way you act toward the person you are picturing.

And once we have done that, I think we have come about as close as we ever will to a definition of what God means by "Love." Our willingness to act in the best interests of someone whom we know perfectly well would not be willing to do so for us.

So this feast of the Body of Christ calls us to some radical reflection indeed. From now on the extent to which we damage our relationship with any other human being, to that extent we damage our relationship with God as well.

That truth, and our acceptance of it in faith, is the core of Christian morality. And so it is hardly surprising that it is also the core of Christian worship. Every week, every day, the Church celebrates the mystery of our intimacy with God. It is because of the Eucharist that Christian morality is what it is. Christ's words, given in two different places in the Scripture, when he speaks of people and says "Love one another as I have loved you." Later he speaks of the Eucharist and says, "Do with one another what I have done with you." These are not two different commands. They call from us a faith in the same truth.

Tenth Sunday in Ordinary Time

It is difficult to think of any theme in Scripture that is more strongly developed, more pervasive, than the one that ties together these readings this weekend. It is a simple enough idea, very simply put. It is the fact that human beings do remarkably well in answering questions that call for facts. Questions that start with what, where, and when. But we do considerably less well answering questions that begin why, what does it mean?

Only God can answer such questions as those, and unless we are willing to substitute his word for ours, his values for ours, his way of acting for ours, we will inevitably fall short of the truth.

Historically, such a sacrifice of self-reliance has been a difficult one for us to make. The temptation has been that we are quite capable of judging for ourselves what is right and wrong, good and evil, truth and error.

By the time of Hosea, the author of the first reading, the Hebrews had done a fine job of building a religious culture on the basis of the revelation to Moses at Mount Sinai. Their law was complex and detailed, rich in ritual and worship, as well as creed and ethic. They began to put all their confidence in their law, their ability to direct themselves. And as they centered more and more on the reasonable morality of man's design, they fell further and further short of the radical morality of God's design. So, through Hosea and the other prophets, God told the people that he was dissatisfied with their formalism and superficial worship.

61

The prophets effected some reform, but not much. By the time Christ began his ministry the bulk of the people were again putting all of their confidence in their human law, their ability to judge the value of ideas and actions and even of people.

And this time they had become so wrapped up in their own ways that when God's ways were again revealed in Christ they were scandalized, angered at what they saw. For Christ not only to talk to a person like Matthew but even to choose him as a friend, an apostle, was a scandal. The law clearly taught that a believer should keep himself free from the company of sinners. And when he is criticized for this kind of behavior, he responds with a quote from Hosea. It is loving kindness that God asks of us, more than any ritual purity. He tells the Pharisees to ponder on that, learn what those words mean.

A willingness to substitute Christ's example for our own judgment, even our own instincts, can only be done through a genuine self-surrender. As St. Paul puts it in the second reading, the self-surrender of faith. Faith, much of the time, means thinking, believing, acting in ways that go beyond reason, if not against it. Faith means following God's ways. And God's ways are not ours.

Eleventh Sunday in Ordinary Time

I suppose there are few feelings more uncomfortable than the feeling of being pointless. It's unsettling because, deep down, we know it's not right. We know that human life is not meant to be pointless. If you look at the characters that are considered great in any society's history, they all really have that one thing in common. They were people with a mission. They had a clear idea of what they had to do, and they set themselves to do it.

We feel attracted to those who seem to have been able to see their lives in the light of the bigger picture, those who have gotten beyond just living from day to day, and have managed to give some real direction to their energies. And we feel that somehow we would like to experience that. We'd like to be in that position, to have a mission, a purpose, a message.

Well, we are in that position, everyone of us. We have been given a message, a message far too big, and far too important to apply simply to each one of us as individuals. We have been given to know some of the most fundamental and basic truths of human nature, and the only way we can respond authentically to those truths is to speak them out clearly and understandably, to pass them on and make them real in the lives of those around us.

The Gospel reading shows that the apostles, those to whom Christ first preached, did not consider themselves any sort of closed community, tightly gathered around the word they had received. Rather, hearing the truth was for them an experience of being sent out, of becoming truly men with a mission. And the first reading, taken from the Old Testament book of Exodus, contains the same idea. It was not enough that the people came to know the fact that God was with them, that they had been saved. The announcement of the truth is followed by a commission, "You shall be to Me a kingdom of priests," a people sent out to mediate this saving presence of God to the rest of the world.

And this is our mission as well. In every contact with Christ that we experience, in Scripture, in Sacraments, in prayer, we are being sent out to bring his presence into all the areas of life in which he is not yet felt. In jobs, in schools, in politics, in family and community living, this message must constantly be repeated, Christ's presence constantly renewed.

We have all been sent by Christ. We have been commissioned by his message of salvation, and we have been pointed toward one another. If the words of the Gospel fail to change and improve our society, it won't be because the message is false. It will be because the messengers never went out.

Twelfth Sunday in Ordinary Time

All three of the Scripture readings selected for today seem to me to focus on one element of the Christian response that to my mind is particularly worthy of attention. And that element simply enough is confidence. A fairly calm, peaceful, even joyous acceptance of whatever it is that the unfolding of our lives may have in store for us.

No matter what the situation may be in which we find ourselves, we must never give in to the temptation to let our experience be the one standard by which we judge the meaning, the value of that situation. We must, rather, be constantly open to a higher meaning, another interpretation that may not agree at all with what our experience has been. And for the authors of these three readings today there is no doubt at all as to just what this unknowable force at work in our lives may be. It is the hand of God protecting, directing, guiding our lives along the lines of his plan for the development of humankind.

That's easy enough to believe when our experience of a situation is a pleasant one. Pleasant experiences fit in very readily with our notion of what God's plan should be. However, that's not the case when our experience of a situation is unpleasant, painful, or even tragic, it can become very difficult indeed to see God's plan at work, very difficult to experience the confidence of which the scriptural authors speak.

And I think there are two steps toward making such a beginning.

The first step is to resist the temptation to write the script. The temptation to play God by mapping out ahead of time just what his plan should be, along what lines humanity should develop. That is true of our interaction with other human beings, and it is certainly true of our interaction with God. This is a difficult step because it involves living always in the presence of mystery.

The second step is to resist the temptation to expect God to act in our lives in the same way as do the other forces we experience around us. The presence of God is a very different sort of force. Its effects are experienced not from the outside, but from within. God's protective hand which so encouraged Jeremiah in the first reading is seen not so much in what goes into making up the situation in which we find ourselves, but rather in the way in which human beings react to, cope with, and ultimately overcome the situation, however challenging or demanding it might be.

In the gospel Christ speaks to us some of his most appealing words. They are simply "Don't be afraid. You will not be destroyed." No matter what happens, humankind, and each individual human person can and will if they choose, at a time and in a way that we simply cannot predict, overcome.

Thirteenth Sunday in Ordinary Time

In today's Gospel the opening line is almost harsh sounding. "Anyone who loves father or mother, son or daughter more than me is not worthy of me." It almost sounds as though Christ were proposing some sort of conflict or opposition between our relationship with God and our human relationships, even those closest and most significant in our lives.

But certainly there is no necessary conflict between our human relationships and our relationship with God. In fact, the quality that marks our relationships with other people is, in fact, the quality that marks our relationship with God. There is a very sacred nature to the bonds of family and friendship, and we must very carefully nurture the strength and intimacy of those bonds.

I think the point is that Christ is urging on us here, as he does so many other places in the Gospel, a true sense of proportion, the ability to distinguish accurately between what matters and what doesn't.

For any number of reasons, perhaps even quite unconsciously, we can find ourselves attaching tremendous weight to really very unimportant things.

Part of the process, I think, of avoiding such distortion is learning to recognize the difference between one's needs and one's wants. Needs must be met. That is every human being's natural right, and for anyone to refuse to even try to meet the real needs of another human being is of course seriously immoral. That is so not only toward relatives and friends but toward anyone.

The first reading today underscores how seriously Mosaic Law taught the moral obligation of hospitality. It was not simply charity to feed and house a passing stranger, it was one's duty. No one's rightful needs can be morally ignored.

Wants are a different matter. Wants don't have to be met. Most of the time life would be more pleasant if they were, more enjoyable, and it is a good thing, a loving thing to meet the wants of other people. But if they are not met, nothing really terrible happens.

Ultimately there is only one real need in life. Salvation. It is the only thing that can ever really last. Everything else, even our deepest and most satisfying human relationships, in comparison, become less important. Not unimportant, but less important.

So, by no means at all is Christ calling us to leave behind or turn our back on family and friends. By no means does following Christ mean resigning ourselves to an earthly life of emotionally empty and sterile human relationships. Christ is calling us to a right view of our lives, a balanced view, an honest perspective. He is calling us to the realization that nothing is more important than our relationship with him, simply because it is on that that everything else that is good ultimately depends, and anything, a thing, a person, a relationship that endangers that is simply not worth doing.

Fourteenth Sunday in Ordinary Time

Scriptural scholars call this Gospel passage the "Hymn of Jubilation" because in it Christ quite literally rejoices in the Father's plan for salvation. He praises the Father's decision to hide himself from the learned and the clever and reveal the greatest truths first to the merest children. The word that is translated here as "children" means literally "the little ones." And it refers not so much to age as to status, the poor, the unimportant, the weak, those who are most certainly not the movers and shakers, the shapers of society.

Now certainly ignorance, in any field, is not a good thing. Quite the contrary, it is a thing to be combatted, erased. For centuries the Church has insisted on the value of learning, of the best possible scholarship.

In the same way neither is it a good thing to starve . . . to have no clothes, no shelter. We completely misunderstand Christ's identification with the poor if we allow ourselves to grow indifferent to the great suffering that poverty causes.

Meekness and humility are hardly virtues if we use them as a way to hide from responsibility, an excuse for doing nothing, never involving oneself in the God-given mission to create the world, to make something good of it.

Rather, Christ praises a sense of poverty, of "littleness," that makes us realize that ultimately there isn't very much difference between having much and having nothing much. That whatever we have it is never really ours, it is from God, and sooner or later will have to be given back to him.

Christ praises a sense of meekness and humility that teaches us not to deny our powers and skills, not to retreat from them, but teaches us rather not to make more of them than they really are. Not to become so taken up with what we can do by our design, that we lose sight of what we must do, by God's design. That is the littleness that saves, that ultimate reliance on God, and a readiness to be directed by his will, even when, especially when, that may seem, for no good reason at all, to contradict our own.

And of course the great thing is that it works. Reliance on God brings happiness. In the last few lines of the Gospel Christ promises, "Do what I do, be little, as I am, and you will find peace. My yoke is easy, my burden is light." Once a person learns that sort of humility and simply stops trying to be influential, powerful, capable, once a person stops trying to direct the flow of people and things and events, something which can't be done anyway, a real burden of anxiety is lifted. For such a person, as for Christ in the Gospel, no matter what else may be going on, suddenly there is room enough in one's life for rejoicing.

Fifteenth Sunday in Ordinary Time

One of the things that always strikes me as I read through the Gospels is how close a parallel there so frequently is between the teaching of the Gospel and the most basic principles of common sense emotional and mental health.

Just the simple fact that, emotionally at least, each one of us lives in the world that we build for ourselves, that ultimately no one can make us feel anyway at all, not happy, not sad, not satisfied, not frustrated. We are, each of us, ultimately, inescapably responsible for the course of our own lives and the emotional flavor of those lives.

Today's Gospel reading is probably one of the clearest instances of that message in all of Scripture. The action of God, the spreading of the seed, was of equal force in each case described. The one thing that made the difference between success or failure from place to place, or from person to person, was the openness, the willingness of the one that received the seed, the Word.

That is a very simple message, really. There is nothing, no system, no person, no thing, that will remove the personal challenge of growth and present us with satisfaction as a finished product, all wrapped up and ready to enjoy.

Here are a few things that nobody packages, things which demand a personal involvement in their own creative processes.

Morality. No one can really teach morality to anyone else. We can and must offer an understanding of the difference between right and wrong in any number of situations. But if that is ever to become something more than simply a list of dos and don'ts, a fundamental goodness must be created and nurtured in each individual.

A sense of purpose. There is no one who can convince any of us that our individual lives are worthwhile, if we are unwilling to create that purpose ourselves.

A sense of identity. It is almost fashionable to spend a lot of time and energy agonizing over the question, "Who am I? Who is the real me?" There is only one answer to that, and it is the same for everyone. Who do you want to be? We are what we do.

Faith. Actually, a lot of things could fit in here. It is easy for us to believe that it is the role of the Church to provide us with faith, in about the same way a grocer provides us with food. Faith doesn't depend on the Church, or on it's leaders, or it's practices, or anything else. Faith depends on God's word being taken in to one's life, taking root there.

As the Gospel says, the seed has been sown, and it continues to be, every day of our lives. There is no guarantee that it will grow. But there is the promise that if we want it to, it can.

Sixteenth Sunday in Ordinary Time

In this Gospel passage Christ speaks to one of the most per-plexing mysteries of human living, the mystery of evil. All of us base our sense of the purposefulness of life on the fundamental moral assumption that the good are rewarded, the evil are pun-ished.

And so, when we look around us and see that so many times, in the imagery of the Gospel, the weeds seem to be doing better than the wheat, that can be a very threatening thing.

Today's Gospel is the answer to the mystery of evil, even if not yet a very satisfying one. The mystery of the tension between good and evil in our world, how the two can exist side by side in a divinely created world, like the weeds and the wheat in the Gospel, is really in essence the mystery of creation. The tension between good and evil is not yet resolved because, simply enough, creation is not yet finished. It is not really true to say that God has created a good world. It is much truer to say that God is cre-ating a good world, that right now the process of creation is going on.

The moral challenge of Christianity is to learn to live lovingly in a world that is right now very often illogical, unjust, even evil, not only because of what it is now, but because of what it is meant to, and will, become.

And this Gospel passage, as well as any number of others, is pretty insistent on the fact that it is God who is the author of this final justice. He will perfect what he has begun.

73

So it is not up to us to combat evil or to punish sinners. We are just not very good at that, really. Every time Christianity has set out to actively fight evil, it has made a horrible mess of things. From the suffocating moral censorship of Puritanism to the carnage of the Crusades and the Inquisition to the bitter hatred of the Counter-Reformation, all of our best efforts at actively eliminating evil in the world have proven to be more of an obstacle than an aid to God's creative process.

Ours is an unfinished world, a world that is still being made. Since the moment God first said, "Let there be light," he has never stopped saying it. The process of creation goes on, and it sweeps us with it. If we struggle against that sweep, if we set our own designs in place of God's, the outcome will inevitably be tragic. No one of us, no whole society of us, has more creative power than God. But if we cooperate with the sweep of creation, if we simply be as God has meant us to be, it will be a joy, and the final justice of God will be well begun in us.

Seventeenth Sunday
in Ordinary Time

Storytelling was a common way of teaching at the time of Christ. Only a very few of the people could read and write, so learning of any kind was largely a matter of memorizing vast amounts of information, and the story form, the concrete images made that a lot easier to do.

The images used by Christ this weekend mean to tell us just one thing really about the Kingdom, and that is that it is good. It is valuable, we should be striving for it. So much so that we should be willing, if need be, to sacrifice everything to become a part of it.

To seek the Kingdom means to accept God's design in place of our own, even without understanding why, even when that design seems not to make life very satisfying but instead seems to make it pretty frustrating.

And it is perfectly true that some of God's design just doesn't seem very satisfying at first glance. When we find ourselves offended, it is hard to see how turning the other cheek could be very satisfying. Common sense would seem to indicate that finding some way to clobber him back would be infinitely more satisfying. It is hard to see how taking one more job, one more responsibility, could be more satisfying than saying something like, "I've done more than my share. It's time for some of those lazy bums out there to shoulder some of the burden." It is hard to see how doing with less materially could possibly be more satisfying than gaining more. It is hard to see how the practice of self-discipline could be more satisfying than giving in to every impulse that is felt. And on and on.

The value of a gigantic pearl is self-evident. It can be measured and weighed, and once a person has seen the possibility of owning it, it is not too difficult for him to convince himself of the wisdom of sacrificing some smaller goods in order to get hold of the big one. That, after all, is just common sense.

Well, the Kingdom of God is not self-evident. It cannot be measured and weighed. It has little enough to do with common sense. That is why God's invitation is called revelation, and our response is called faith. A share in the Kingdom of God is not built in a laboratory, where effect always follows cause, where precise technique yields precise results. Rather, that share is pieced together in a very confusing world where the virtues of trust, faithfulness, forgiveness, and love are the only techniques that really work.

We may not understand God's design, but we can act on it. And if we do, we have found the pearl of great price in the Gospel. And the satisfaction that comes with being in possession of that final good, the best that life has to offer, will be ours.

Eighteenth Sunday
in Ordinary Time

I suppose one of the biggest challenges that faces anyone in the process of growing up emotionally is that of learning to trust. It is such a simple sounding word but such an enormously complex reality, and integrating trust into our lives in a healthy adult sort of way can be a challenge indeed.

There is a good deal that goes into making up such a trust. It has to include a presumption of goodness in others. It has to include a presumption of ability in others. And it has to include a certain surrender of control over one's own circumstances.

I think it was Gabriel Marcel who once wrote that there is a difference between hope and expectations. Expectations, he said, are in terms of particular projects, particular outcomes, a definite, detailed plan for what should or should not be. And as such they are necessarily a narrowing thing, they tie us down to too small a world, too small a range of choices. But hope is simply an unconditional trust that God will lead us lovingly, and for the best, in any setting. A trusting hope urges us to set aside, in a sense, our own definition of what is good and bad, acceptable or not, and take on instead God's, even when that is not very clear to us sometimes.

One of my favorite images in Scripture is lodged in this Gospel reading for today. Some of the apostles tell Christ that he had better start to wrap up whatever it was he was doing as the day is coming to an end, and the thousands of people gathered about him are going to need to find themselves something to eat before nightfall. And Christ's response to that is, "Let's feed them ourselves. Tell the people to sit down." Now, it's not too difficult to imagine the apostles standing there with polite smiles on their faces, looking at each other and thinking, perhaps not too quietly, "Now that is about the dumbest idea I ever heard. This simply won't work." But being respectful men, the most they say is something like, "Perhaps it's escaped your attention, but we don't have anything to give them. We only have five loaves of bread, and a few fish, and that is really not even enough for the twelve of us." And Christ responds, "It doesn't have to make sense. Most of life doesn't. Just do as I ask."

And of course it was only after the twelve baskets were filled with the leftovers that the apostles really saw what had happened. It is only in hindsight that we can clearly see God's care for us. That is another reason for suspending judgment now. A Christian has all of eternity to use hindsight. When we finally can look back on our lives and see clearly how God has led us, it will be from the vantage point of God himself.

Nineteenth Sunday
in Ordinary Time

There is a story that once a visitor came to St. Teresa of Avila and asked, "How should I picture God when I pray? What about him is most real?" And her answer was simply enough, "Picture him looking at you."

I don't know if the visitor was satisfied with that answer, but he should have been. Christ is indeed looking at us, at each one of us. His knowledge of each of us is personal, his concern for each of us is personal, and his call to each of us is personal. He can be found, recognized, and responded to.

This Gospel reading for this weekend, is an eloquent treatment of just that notion. In so many places in Scripture the sea, a stormy, unruly sea, is used as a symbol of the world, life, without God. The apostles have been separated from Christ, they are alone in their boat, and the sea, the world without Christ, is stormy and chaotic indeed. So much so that they are about to be overcome by it. Then Christ is pictured as mastering the storm. He literally walks over it.

Peter saw Christ looking at him through the storm, and became confident that together with Christ, he, too, would be able to overcome the chaos that seemed to surround him. Peter said, "Lord, tell me to come to you." And so he did, he held out his hand to Peter.

And here Matthew describes beautifully something at least of what St. Paul would later call the contradiction, the foolishness of

Christianity. Before you can walk on the water, you gotta get out of the boat. Before Peter could benefit from Christ's power, he would have to step out of whatever had been holding him up until then, he would have to risk walking away from what seemed to be so safe and secure and reasonable.

And for us, too, that is the hard part. Getting out of the boat. Putting aside the false dependencies, the securities, all the ways that we think we can make ourselves immune from chaos. Materialism is a popular boat. What could be a better barrier against the chaos than money and the things and the power it can buy. Any number of dependencies can float us along for a while. Drugs, alcohol, pleasure, acceptance. Even the human relationships in our lives can be a dependency, an influence that keeps us from hearing Christ's call. So can laziness, the habits we build of not responding, not involving ourselves. So can fear, perhaps even more commonly.

Matthew's intricate symbolism this weekend is clear and eloquent. Christ is very near. He is standing at the edge of our own personal storm, calling us. But in order to respond we must ignore the storm, look down at the boat, name it, and climb out.

Twentieth Sunday in Ordinary Time

The Gospel reading for today gives us what to my mind is one of the strangest images of Christ in all of Scripture. In fact he even seems, at first, to be outright offensive. Christ is approached by a woman whose daughter is ill. And she, as hundreds of others had done, asked Christ for his help to cure the girl.

But Christ says to the woman, "My concern is not with you. Only with the people of Israel." But the woman does not give up, she presses her plea. And then Christ says something that seems very harsh. He says, "It would not be right for me to take something that belongs to God's chosen people, the Jews, the sons and daughters, and throw it to the dogs, to someone like you."

The woman was a Canaanite, a member of one of the tribes that the Jews had conquered when they took over the Promised Land. And that ugliest of human emotions, outright prejudice, was the force at work in this Gospel scene. In the minds of the apostles, the woman was not one of the chosen people, she was not "one of us," and as such she had no right to even make a request of God, let alone assume that he would do anything about it. And so Christ's attitude, the role that he seems to be playing, was really much more directed toward the apostles than it was toward the woman. By himself being so much a man of his time and culture, by recognizing, even verbalizing, the prejudicial attitude of his followers, Christ sort of picks up this intolerance and holds it up in front of their faces and, then, by his final loving acceptance of the woman, condemns it, contradicts it, begins to turn it around.

But the smug, self-satisfied righteousness of the Hebrews was a deeply ingrained thing, and the controversy between those who believed that Christianity should be a sect of Judaism, such as Peter, at first, and those who believed that the Church must move to the world, open new horizons, be in fact missionary.

I suppose that that word, "missionary," for most of us, conjures up exotic images of South America, or Africa, or Asia. It is too bad that the word doesn't sometimes conjure up images of our own dinner tables, our own living rooms, our schools, our business places, the streets of our own town. There is a great deal of missionary work to be done right in our own community. To be missionary means to find the places where Christ is not known, or not known well, and to bring him there. And doing that is not the kind of missionary work that is done by teaching Christianity. Rather that is the kind of missionary work that is done by being Christian.

Twenty-First Sunday
in Ordinary Time

The first reading and the Gospel for today are pretty similar. Isaiah says what God's appointed shall shut, no one shall open, what he shall open, no one shall shut. In the Gospel, Matthew says of God's appointed, "You are the Rock. You have the keys to the Kingdom. Whatever you close shall be closed, whatever you open shall be opened."

And when those of us who hear those words ask, as we certainly do, "Why? Why would the Lord choose to put a simple and imperfect human being in such a position of power and responsibility?" the second reading offers a very unsatisfying answer. And that is simply, "The Lord has his own ways. He alone can see the final purpose to his unfolding plan."

The Gospel reading is one of the passages that is traditionally used to establish and to demonstrate the role of the papacy in the Catholic Church. Peter, in his response to Christ's questioning, demonstrates the clearest understanding of who Christ is and what he has come to accomplish. And based on this Christ commissions Peter to fill his role, to be for the people, as much as he could, what Christ had shown himself to be. Peter, like Christ, was to be the center point of God's people, to form the people around himself, to give them a cohesiveness, a direction, a real history, much as Moses and Abraham had been called to form the history of the people of Israel around themselves.

And this is what gives a living meaning to the word "sacrament," the enfleshing of the working of grace in human beings, the things that they use, the things that they do. It is an emphasis that is made itself felt in every aspect of our lives as Catholics, from papal teaching to the role of the bishop, the administration of sacraments, the formation of a Christian atmosphere in the community and in the home, the righting of whatever wrongs there may be in the social order, and so on. The emphasis on the fact that God's work, if it is to be done, is to be done by human beings.

Why listen when the pope teaches? Why come together, surround ourselves with other people, as we do this morning to worship in this formal, ritualized way? Why confess to a human being? Why work at building up a sense of moral responsibility in our dealing with other human beings? Why try to save the world, or even make it just a little better? Why not just admit that ultimately these are things that only God can handle? Because that is true. Only God can. And he will. The challenge for us is to grasp how he has chosen to handle them. And the answer is clear. Through human beings. Through us, through our human abilities, human efforts. Christ has said it. "I entrust to you the keys of the Kingdom."

Twenty-Second Sunday in Ordinary Time

I suppose that if a person were to search all through the Scriptures trying to find a couple of passages that make Christianity sound like a dangerous business, we really couldn't do much better than to settle on these readings for today.

The first is from the personal writings of the Old Testament prophet Jeremiah. With a voice as cutting as any in Scripture he calls the people to stop hiding from the reality of their comfortable lives, face up to their failings, their sin, and do something about it, become again the people of God.

And for that Jeremiah was an outcast. He was ridiculed, even persecuted, by those whom he confronted with the truth.

And the Gospel, too, has much of that same demanding quality to it. Here Christ begins to introduce to his apostles the idea of his death. But Peter objected. It was not going to be that way.

Christ reacts very sharply to Peter. But it was necessary. Peter, perhaps more than any of the others, had to understand what was happening, had to see the point to it, the value.

And then Christ explains his response, but in a puzzling, enigmatic sort of way, almost with a kind of a riddle. Whoever wants to save his life will lose it, whoever loses his life for me will save it. If anyone wants to follow me, he can do so only by carrying the cross that I carry.

So again there seems to be almost that sense of a harshness to the practice of God's values. That sense that Christianity, if you do it right, has to hurt.

Nothing could be further from the truth. God calls us not to suffering and pain but to happiness, a joy, a feeling of rightness to our lives. And it is an absolute promise, there is no "maybe" attached to it. It is a sure and certain thing.

But if the promise is absolute, it is by no means unconditional. Nowhere does God promise us, "You will be happy and satisfied, no matter what you do, no matter how you live." The promise is given to those who accept no standard other than Christ's, who do not compromise with the truth, even if that means a cross of one kind or another.

And that is the point. Purposefulness. The fact is that a very great deal of the burdens that mark our lives have nothing at all to do with the cross. They are of human origin. We make them ourselves, by centering our lives on something less than the truth, something less than real value.

A burden, a hardship in our lives is a cross, if it has a purpose, if it leads somewhere, if it leads to a resurrection. That after all is what most clearly marks the cross of Christ.

Twenty-Third Sunday
in Ordinary Time

The Gospel this weekend addresses the issue of the conflict that can arise from time to time because of the interdependence of his people.

Christ is pictured as discussing just such a question with his apostles and proposing to them a method of resolution. He says, "Suppose that someone has offended you, that you have a real grievance against another. What should you do?" And Christ's first advice is simply, "Tell that person about it." Bring it up, talk about it.

But then he adds a very important note. To begin with at least, keep it private. Try to resolve it where it exists, between the individuals involved.

But that private confrontation may not work. And Christ's advice here is consistent. Don't stop, don't pull back. If damage is still being done, concern and involvement cannot be withheld. He says, "Call in a witness or two."

And then the next step, the next two steps that Christ proposes, ring a bit harshly. He says that if that doesn't work, refer the matter to the Church. In effect, make it public. And if even that doesn't work, then back off, in a sense, from that person. Alter, even drastically alter, the nature of the relationship that generates conflict.

Making it public means that if a situation in which damage is being done cannot be resolved privately, then it is no longer a private situation. It does mean that those whose charge it is to preserve whatever values are being damaged must be involved. If it is a civil value, then civil authority; community value, then community authority. If the health of a person, be it physical or emotional is the value, then those agencies must be involved. For anyone of us to simply sit back and watch anyone of us damage themselves or others is sinful.

And then finally, Christ says that we may have to radically alter the nature of our relationship to the person or situation that is generating the conflict if nothing else works.

Now, that never means that we withdraw from anyone our concern, or our readiness to become involved in their well-being. But it does mean that when all else has been tried, we may come to a point at which we simply have to say, "I am not going to co-operate in any way with the damage that is being done. I am not going to help it be done, not even passively, not to me, nor to anyone else." In the extreme, it may even mean simply no longer associating with that individual.

Human interdependence is not simple. Whether it be a matter of supporting the good we see in others or correcting the faults, we cannot, as a Christian, live behind a wall. The people we are called to serve are on the other side of that wall. And because they are there, so is God.

Twenty-Fourth Sunday
in Ordinary Time

The Scripture readings for today lay out for us a quality that is perhaps as much as any other, unmistakably Christian, even uniquely Christian. And that is the quality, the virtue of forgiveness.

The teaching of the Gospel is pretty clear. Peter questions Christ as to how much is enough? Where is the breaking point? Just how far is a person reasonably expected to go with forgiveness?

And Christ's answer is simply, "There are no limits." The quality of forgiveness is to be brought into play just as often as it is needed. The Hebrews of Christ's time made wide use of numbers as symbols, and for a wide range of reasons, seven was a mystical number, the number of limitless perfection. So to multiply something by seven meant to remove the limits from that something, to place it on a spiritual plane.

And that is so because no matter what we are asked to forgive one another, it is nothing compared to the forgiveness that God is constantly willing to offer us. Really, the Father's constant readiness to forgive is the reason why we are called to forgive one another. Forgiveness is never a business deal. I'll forgive you if you do such and such. It is simply there, asking of us only that we accept it. In the same way the forgiveness, the opportunity for reconciliation that we offer to one another, can never be a business deal. There are no ifs, no conditions. We must offer it to others as freely and as lovingly as it is offered to us.

I think that one of the problems that a lot of people have with this quality, the virtue of forgiveness, is really just not knowing what it means. So often we can find ourselves in the position of saying, "I know I should forgive so and so, but I just can't put it out of my mind."

Well, really, forgiveness has nothing much to do with putting something out of your mind. As with any virtue, forgiveness is not primarily a way you feel. It is primarily a decision you make. A decision to the effect that I will not let an injury I have received be the motive for the way that I will act toward the one who has hurt me. I won't let what has been done to me dictate or color the way that I act toward that person.

Our readiness to forgive one another is a clear and dependable measure of our readiness to accept Christian revelation as a model for life. And it is not beyond the reach or the ability of any one of us. Because each of us has more than likely already been forgiven far more than we shall ever be asked to forgive.

Twenty-Fifth Sunday
in Ordinary Time

The Gospel reading for today can be a puzzling one. It was for the people of Christ's own time as well.

They had for centuries put their faith in a God who dealt with his people in a very precise and predictable way, a God who set down the terms of his relationship to his people in a very clear form, the terms of the Law, a law that guaranteed in an almost measurable way, a reward for merit, and a punishment for sin. And that just, reliable God was pretty much the model the people were to use in their relationships with one another. An eye for an eye and a tooth for a tooth was the ethic of the time.

And so it was hard for them to understand the kind of person of whom Christ speaks in the Gospel when he describes the master of the vineyard, a person so generous that he almost seems to offend our normal standards of justice. But yet that is the picture, the model of God that Christ presents. A picture of a God whose generosity, whose concern for our welfare does not depend strictly and precisely on what we do for him, but rather on what he wills to do for us.

And I suppose one of the reasons why we have such a difficult time understanding the generosity of God is simply because, so often, generosity is such a foreign thing in our own lives. This parable is disturbing to the kind of people who are constantly agonizing over whether or not they are being treated fairly, whether or not they are getting everything they have got coming, whether it be money, recognition, power, acceptance. It is disturbing to the kind of people who constantly measure what they have and are against what others have and are, the kind of people who consider it an outrage, a tragedy, if someone else ever seems to come out ahead, get the better of them, take advantage of them, even just a little.

On the other hand, this parable is not in the least disturbing. It makes great sense to those who can say with Paul in the second reading that to live means to toil for the sake of others. This parable makes great sense to those who realize that no other human being, what they have, what they are, can ever possibly be a valid yardstick to be used in measuring one's own well-being. It makes sense to those who are willing to give far more of themselves than what they feel others deserve simply because they know that that is what a Christian is called to do, and because they know that however great their own generosity, it will seem pretty skimpy compared to that of the Father.

Twenty-Sixth Sunday
in Ordinary Time

Throughout the Gospel there is one type of person that invariably seems to provoke Christ's anger, that never seems to merit a good word from Christ, only his scorn and his condemnation. And that is the group of people the Gospel authors usually refer to as the Pharisees. But when Christ criticizes he isn't talking about a political party or a social class. Rather he is talking about an attitude, a way of life, one that seemed very often to be typical of the Pharisees.

It was an attitude that was characterized by two vices. Hypocrisy and self-righteousness. A hypocrite is a person that is more concerned with a good image than a good conscience. A person who works very hard at playing a role, creating an impression, but who really holds very few deep convictions. And a self-righteous person is a hypocrite who takes himself very seriously, a hypocrite who has really become cut off from the possibility of growth because of the belief that the role that is being played, the image that is being built, is in fact something worthwhile and valuable.

So it is the superficiality, the moral and spiritual emptiness of the Pharisees, that offended Christ and the fact that they had become so smugly self-satisfied with that emptiness.

And I think that sets the scene, really, for this Gospel reading for today. In the parable that Christ uses, in the contrast between the first and second son, he really compares the morality of the

Pharisees, the self-righteous hypocrites with that of the sinners, and finds it wanting. Compared to the sinners who recognized their faults and tried to do something about them, the static, unmoving Pharisees were dead, dry, empty creatures. Now, obviously enough, it is not the sin of the idolaters and prostitutes that Christ is praising, rather it is their awareness, their effort at growth, even if that effort is unsuccessful for awhile. It is almost as if to say that it is not so much on our sin that Christ judges us but rather on how satisfied we are with our sin. How complacent we are, how attached to it we become. In his association with sinners, Christ saw beyond their sin and saw what the Pharisees couldn't, or wouldn't. In their effort, in their attempts to remake their lives, in their repentance, Christ saw goodness and virtue.

And I think there is a comfort in that for us. Or there should be. Just as Christ praised and blessed with his company, saw virtue in the halting, faulty effort at growth of the idolaters and prostitutes, so will he in our own. That all means there is only one real sign of hopelessness in our lives, and that is to give up, to quit trying, to be satisfied with what we are. The only thing that should ever make us despair of the company of Christ is our refusal to accept it. We don't have to make ourselves perfect. We can't. Only Christ can do that. But he will. As long as we keep trying to make ourselves better.

Twenty-Seventh Sunday
in Ordinary Time

Both the first reading from the Old Testament book of the prophet Isaiah and the Gospel reading present us with examples of one of the commonest images, I suppose, in all of Scripture, that of the vineyard and the one who cares for it.

And the point of the image is pretty clear. It is to illustrate the care, the concern, that the Father lavishes on us, his people. We have not been called together to be left on our own. Rather we have been called together to benefit from the direction, the purpose, the meaning that the Father can and will give to our lives.

It is simply true that part at least of the frustration that seems to characterize the lives of a great many people today is really a kind of a sense of being set adrift in a world in which we are faced with far greater demands, challenges than any of us are capable of meeting. Whether the task be making a living, making peace, finding justice, raising a family, finding a friend, or simply doing one's job, an awful lot of people experience themselves as facing it alone, as more than they can handle.

Well, the scriptural response to this is very clear. It is not so. There is no challenge, no task, no life that any of God's people are asked to face entirely alone. Our concerns are the Father's concerns. Our efforts to grow are under his care, his direction. It is simply his understanding of this that enables Paul in the second reading to say, "Dismiss all anxiety from your minds. Present your needs to the Father, and his own peace will stand guard over you."

But we must remember that the image of the vineyard is just that, an image. It tells part of the story, not all of it. And the rest of the story is that we, the Church, are not plants, we are people. And that means that our role, our responsibility, can never be to simply sit back and let someone else, even the owner, do all the work, take care of us. Plants don't need to become personally involved in the gardener's mission in order to grow. People do. Paul tells us, "Don't be anxious. Don't despair." He does not tell us, "Don't be concerned, don't be involved in your own growth."

We must come to see God's presence, his care, his direction as an invitation, an opportunity, for our own active, responsible involvement in our own personal growth, not as a substitute for it. We must see God's presence as a call to growth, not as a guarantee of it. The image of the vineyard is a valuable one. It offers us a valuable confidence, a real freedom from anxiety. But let us remember that in this image we are not only the vine, we are the caretakers as well.

Twenty-Eighth Sunday
in Ordinary Time

There is a wealth of meaning carried by the imagery used in today's first reading and Gospel. The image of the Kingdom of God as a meal. The power of that image was much more evident, I would imagine, to the people of Isaiah's or Christ's time, than it is to our own. They had not yet sacrificed the notion of a meal to the taco stand or drive-in. The people of Isaiah's and Christ's time still held very intensely to the notion of the meal as a drama, a document, in which the whole of their lives, the quality of those lives was acted out, expressed, and affirmed. The feast celebrated on the mountain in Isaiah, the wedding feast in the Gospels, in a word, a meal done well, experienced rightly, all of that is life as God intended it to be, life done well, acted out rightly.

When life is right, when it is marked by right understanding, right relationships, the meal is right. But when that is not the case, when righteousness fails, the meal is disrupted, the document is distorted. The verses in Isaiah just prior to this reading speak to the corruption of the covenant, the infidelity of the people. And Isaiah describes it as a hunger in the people. He says, "In the streets they cry out for lack of wine. . . ." The almost harsh sounding imagery of the guest who is thrown out in the Gospel because he would not dress properly strikes the same note. The issue is not proper dress, the issue is the disruption of the meal, refusing to do it right, refusing to accept the right relationship between himself and the host, and to do so on the host's terms. Perhaps that is really the heart of the imagery. Do we come to the meal on our own terms, or on those of the host? Do we write the document that expresses our lives, or does God?

I think this imagery could be pursued for a long time. It is a rich one, both in Scripture and in human experience. But there is a disturbing side to doing so. If something very ancient and very deep within us makes of a meal a document that speaks of the quality of our lives, what is being said by what our culture makes of meals? The speed of them, the superficiality? How many families do we know that eat together, all together, same time, same place, more than perhaps once a week? What is added to the document of our lives by the fact that we spend more on remedies for indigestion than many nations spend on food?

The invitation to the banquet that is given us is an invitation to nothing less than life itself, life as God means it to be. And that, if done rightly, is a thing to celebrate.

Twenty-Ninth Sunday
in Ordinary Time

There is something about the kind of prophecy being offered in the first reading this weekend that always seems just a little farfetched, even strained. But perhaps it doesn't really matter whether or not God actually hand-picked Cyrus and sent him, purposefully, into Persia as a savior for the Israelites. Perhaps all that matters is that in that event the people affected saw meaning and acted on that meaning. They not only went home, they did so renewed, rededicated to the Law, firmly resolved to never again let the presence of God go unnoticed in their midst.

History, the flow of human events, is God's. But it is his not in that he manipulates the characters and events of history like puppets on a string, but rather in that he empowers his people to grow, to flourish, to become more and more his own, no matter what happens to them. The question for believers, in response to any movement of history, worldwide, or simply one's own, is not "Why did God do this?" but rather, "What does he want me to do in the wake of it?"

That was something of the challenge faced by Christ as he verbally fenced with the Pharisees and Herodians, two parties normally at each other's throats. Their question, "Is it right for us to pay the Roman tax, or not?" was a loaded one. The flattery with which it is introduced was not sincere. If he said "Yes," he would seem to be accepting the legitimacy of Roman domination as God's will and would alienate the many and zealous Zionists in Israel. If

99

he said "No," he would be identifying his mission as just another of a long stream of political revolutionary movements, the sort of thing with which the Romans knew how to deal very well.

Christ's response is an invitation to his listeners to clarify their vision of God's design and their conviction that such a design is in fact God's. The Kingdom of God and the Kingdom of Caesar are both real; it would be foolish to pretend otherwise. That reality must be recognized and adapted to. But they are nowhere near of equal import, equal power. The fact is that the Kingdom of God, if it is clearly envisioned, keenly desired, can and will flourish under any political or economic conditions, be that exile in Babylon, under harsh Roman domination, or anywhere else.

The Kingdom of God, and its growth, has very little to do with to whom one pays taxes, under what sort of political system or on what economic level one lives. The fortunes of politics and economics come and go. There have been a thousand Babylons and Cyruses, and there will be a thousand more. But the virtues of the Kingdom must be constant and unchanging if they are of the Kingdom of God. If they are, then even from Babylon and Cyrus, something Godly can be drawn.

Thirtieth Sunday in Ordinary Time

There is probably nothing that a person can do that can so quickly bring to the surface all of one's most deeply rooted insecurities and self-doubts as can watching a few TV commercials. The fact is that all of those small anxieties over how we look and feel and smell spring from a much larger one, one to which every human being ever born is subject. And that is, "What do people think of me?" To put it all in a word, "Am I really lovable?"

We need to be appreciated, to be loved. The experience of loving and being loved is really the touchstone of human life. It is what makes life worth living, and it is ultimately the only thing that does so.

In the Gospel reading for today Christ speaks to the centrality of love in human life. He says that love is not only the key to a satisfying human life, it is also the only way to be saved.

The Pharisees try to draw Christ into an argument by asking him which is the greatest, the most binding of all the laws. And the first part of his answer was expected. Love God first, always, and above everything else. But the second half of his answer was pretty unexpected. Love your neighbor as yourself. Certainly love of neighbor was not a new idea to the Hebrews. What was new was the importance that Christ gave to that commandment. Christ virtually draws a parallel between the love of God and the love of neighbor. To say that the second commandment is like the first is to say that what one does to people, one does to God.

Really, I suppose, love will never be "understood" . . . it is, after all, a mystery. We may not be able to say definitively what love is, but we can say a great deal about what it is like. We can say that it is free . . . it is a free gift of self, given to another, for the good of that other. Love is not a contract or a business deal . . . "I will love you if you do such and such for me." It is a free gift.

And that means that love is not a need. That kind of stance is something much closer to dependence than to a free gift of self. It is nice to be needed, but it is much better to be loved.

Contrary to the popular saying, love is not blind. Or it shouldn't be. It should see not only with the eyes of the senses and of the mind but with the eyes of faith. It should see below the surface, to the essential dignity and infinite value of every human being.

It is a complex thing, this commandment that Christ gives us, to love one another and in so doing to love God. It may take us a lifetime, even more than a lifetime, to get it right.

Thirty-First Sunday in Ordinary Time

The Pharisees to whom Christ is speaking in this passage were a class of people very learned in the Law, very skilled at its interpretation.

They knew very well that it was being just such guardians of the Law that guaranteed their position. And so, slowly, over centuries, the base of their power, that on which they relied, became not their love of the Law, but their knowledge of it, their ability to manipulate it.

And manipulate it they did, to the point which Christ describes in this Gospel reading when he says, "You bind up heavy loads, impossible for others to carry . . ." And the heavy load that they had bound up was the Law itself. They did that by writing into the Law itself centuries of legal and theological decisions, policy statements, scriptural interpretation, made in particular situations about particular cases. The Pharisees had become the kind of people whose first concern, when faced with a moral challenge, an issue of virtue, such as that of the woman taken in the act of adultery, would be to surround themselves, protect themselves in the intricacies of the issue. And if there were no intricacies, they would make some. The kind of people who would say, "We need to come up with a comprehensive statement on that. We need to form a study committee to research this."

Christ cuts through all of that with a razor-like simplicity. "No one condemns you, and neither do I. Now don't do that anymore."

It is a disturbing thing, someone who says what they mean, who speaks from the heart, directly, plainly, honestly. Simplicity can be a risky business.

What if Christ really means most of what he says, just as he says it? What if he really meant the Beatitudes? The peacemakers are the children of God. The gentle, the humble, will see God. Those who hunger and thirst for holiness, not power, not position, not wealth, they will be the people of the New Kingdom. What if it is all meant very literally, what if we really are to be judged on what we do, not what we profess? A stumbling block indeed for a Christianity tangled up in its own issues and causes and movements.

Christianity isn't so difficult to discuss, after all. But it can be pretty challenging to live.

Thirty-Second Sunday
in Ordinary Time

Of all the ways that the authors of Scripture could think of to praise their heroes, kings, prophets, judges, it seems that the highest of all was to say of that person that he or she was "wise."

I suppose one of the reasons why we today might find this virtue of Wisdom a little difficult to appreciate is because for us the word has probably lost some of its scriptural sense. When we think of a "wise person" today, the image that comes to mind is probably along the lines of an old man with a long white beard, who has spent the whole of his life locked in a room with his books.

But that really is a far cry from what the scriptural authors mean by Wisdom. In the second reading, for example, Paul counts as wise those who have managed to make some sort of peace with the eminently practical matter of dying. The Gospel speaks of Wisdom simply in terms of the five bridesmaids who had sense enough to realize that the wedding procession may well be delayed, such things often are, and bring along some extra oil for their lamps. At the heart of it, for the scriptural author, people of wisdom are realists. They know the world as it really is. Not necessarily as they would like it to be and not necessarily as others tell them it is.

There is another way to put all that really, a way even more closely reflecting the scriptural author's insight. The wise person is the person who knows what God knows, sees the world as he sees it. In the book of Proverbs the author writes, "The beginning of Wisdom is the fear of the Lord." Well, that's not a very good translation. The word just doesn't mean "fear." Better would be, "The beginning of Wisdom is a submission, an openness to the Lord." A willingness to listen quietly when he speaks. The beginning of Wisdom is to realize that only God can know life as it really is, and so only in his word, in what he reveals to be true, can Wisdom be found.

Knowing what to do, in order to make the best, truly the best, of whatever situation I am in right now. That is living in the real world, and that is Wisdom. But also, never losing sight of the fact that no matter what situation I am in right now, it will change. So never being overwhelmed, overcome, by what happens now, but rather using all of it as a preparation for what will happen then, that, too, is reality, and it is Wisdom. It is the crowning virtue, and, as the book of Proverbs promises, it stirs up in us the ability to take great pleasure in what God has already done for us and great delight in what he has yet to do.

Thirty-Third Sunday
in Ordinary Time

This weekend the Scriptural readings begin to sort of prime us, lead us into the coming Advent experience of waiting. And the readings do this by drawing on part at least of the strong scriptural theme of the end times, the second coming of the Lord, the end of the world.

And it is a very complex, a very mysterious picture of that event that the Scriptures draw. Any number of different images and emphases are used. Powerful, eloquent images, drawn from the daily life of the Hebrews. Images of warfare and a great show of power. Images from farming. The end times will be like a field coming to full fruit, a vineyard that finally bears, or like a shepherd that goes out into the countryside, separates his own sheep from the rest, and brings them back to his own fold. Images from commerce, or court life, images of childbirth.

But from all of that confusion of imagery there does emerge a consistent pattern. There are qualities to that experience that are clearly revealed.

One of those qualities is unpredictability. It will be something that happens on God's terms, in his own time. Paul, in the second reading today, echoes that strong Gospel theme. When and where and how are simply not ours to know.

And that leads to another of the qualities that is revealed, that of clarity. The "not knowing" that we have to bear in so many areas of our life will be eased. In one of his letters Paul writes,

"We see now as though we were looking through a dark glass . . ." but then we shall see everything clearly, as it is.

And that points, I think, to a third quality of the end times that is so clearly scriptural, the quality of judgment. The simple fact is that we have been created by God to be accountable creatures, accountable to him and to one another and that we shall one day be called to give that account, and be held to it.

This Gospel today is one of a couple of Scripture passages that deals with the reality of judgment. And here, as elsewhere, the standard that is used, the yardstick by which a person's life is judged, is not nearly so much the amount of evil he has done as it is the amount of good he did or did not do. The master who returns to judge his servants does so really on the basis of their creativity, their fruitful use of what he has given them, their ability to leave a situation better than it was when they entered it.

When our Master left he gave a commission to each of his servants, "Go out into the whole world, and bring it to me, better than it was." Perhaps the clearest image of all of the end times is simply the question, "How well have we done that?"

Christ the King

It is certainly no accident that the image that is selected for the last Sunday of the liturgical year, the image that is meant to sort of sum up all the others, is that of Christ the King.

For most of us, I suppose, royalty, majesty speaks of the distance between the king and ordinary people, how much unlike other people the king really is.

But for Christ, the title "king" meant just the opposite. Christ is King because his life is so intimately bound up with our own. He is a king who rules from within. He doesn't exercise power; he is power. He doesn't govern the lives of his people; he is the lives of his people. Christ is the Lord of human history because, as Paul puts it in the second reading, it is Christ who draws together all the separate, diverse forces and energies in that history, giving them a single unified purpose, a single, unified direction.

The bond between this king and his people is so total, so intimate, that any act of kindness and acceptance directed toward any one of his people is experienced by Christ himself. Any act of unkindness or of hurt directed toward any one of his people is experienced by Christ himself. And the Gospel clearly expects us to take this quite literally. When Christ says, "What you do to them you do to me," he is not using vague poetic symbols. He is rather revealing to us the deepest reality of all our human interaction, a truth we must take into consideration any time we make a moral judgment, any time we decide how we are going to act in any particular situation. So the moral decision for a Christian is not first

"How should I act toward this or that person?" The question is rather, "How should I act toward Christ himself?"

And it is really only when we do begin to seriously ask that question, when we realize that Christ himself feels our kindness and is hurt by our offenses, only then do our loving deeds become truly Christian. When we finally begin to see Christ as the third party in every contact we have with other people, then we will begin to free ourselves from the need to be repaid for all our goodness, the need to be recognized, honored, and rewarded for all the wonderful things we do. As long as we are bound by that kind of desire our love is not Christian self-giving, it is simply a business deal.

Christ calls each of us to a careful concern for the way we build our lives today, a careful concern for all the people that fill those lives . . . because whatever we do to one of them, we do to him.

AM720 **HOLY FAMILY RADIO** WHYF

Nourishing our Catholic Faith
Sharing our Faith with others

Douglas J. Neatrour

General Manager

8 West Main Street
Shiremanstown, PA 17011
(studio)

717.525.8110 tel • 717.525.8137 fax

www.720whyf.com
contact@720whyf.com